You are now t[...]
for posterit[...]
doesn't bring
bad memories.

Best wishes.

Ken

GW01401173

STEPSONS OF HEAVEN

STEPSONS OF HEAVEN

Ken Taylor

The Book Guild Ltd
Sussex, England

The Book Guild Ltd,
25 High Street,
Lewes, Sussex

First published 1999
© Ken Taylor 1999

Set in Times
Typesetting by IML Typographers, Chester
Printed in Great Britain by
Bookcraft (Bath) Ltd, Avon

A catalogue record for this book is
available from the British Library

ISBN 1 85776 389 0

CONTENTS

vi

'But we must not altogether despair for the sailor; nor need those who toil for his good be at bottom disheartened. For Time must prove his friend in the end; and though sometimes he would almost seem as a neglected step-son of heaven, permitted to run on and riot out his days with no hand to restrain him, while others are watched over and tenderly cared for; yet we feel and we know that God is the true Father of all, and that none of His children are without the pale of His care.'

Redburn, 1839.
Herman Melville.

PREFACE

This is my first attempt to write about my life at sea, which covers a period of some forty-two years, beginning in 1945 just before the end of the Second World War and ending in New Zealand in 1987. The reason for this effort to portray life at sea in merchant ships is because I firmly believe that from reading many books which affected to describe the maritime milieu, there is no factual account of what it was like to sail for a living under the 'Red Duster'.

Thinking about the four decades I spent at sea, I can understand some of the difficulties involved in describing the sheer sordidness of life in many of the floating slums that I have worked aboard in the past.

Primarily there is the problem of the language used aboard ships, the monotonous obscenities which are the *lingua franca* used by seamen, would soon become tedious to the average reader. Although some people would find it amusing I suppose for a certain length of time, it would become somewhat boring for anyone with any claim to intellectual pretensions.

There would also be the problem of the maritime jargon which I suppose would entail the creation of a glossary. It would be very difficult to write about the subject in a consistent manner objectively and this would pose problems to the writer who has lived through the situations described. Many of these are still vividly remembered and still rankle even after many years have passed since they took place.

FOREWORD

This is a semi-biographical account of life at sea in British merchant ships, between the years 1945 and 1987. I have chosen to write about this subject because it is now a way of life that has passed into history, and as far as I can see from reading many books purporting to be about sea life, nobody has written a factual account about what it was like to earn a living working on British merchant vessels over four decades.

I find it a somewhat amazing fact that I lasted so long in the shipping industry, and, being Anglo-Irish, I did not take kindly to discipline. This is probably the basic reason that I chose to go to sea in the first place at the age of seventeen years. At that stage I could see conscription looming on the horizon and realised that Kings Rules and Regulations would not suit my temperament, added to which I had completed a couple of years in the Bolton Sea Cadet Corps during which I sailed for a fortnight on a Motor minesweeper out of Morpeth Dock in Birkenhead in 1944. Fourteen days was all it took me to realise that the flagrant class distinction which prevailed in the Royal Navy at that time, was not for me.

My class conscious attitude was very noticeable even at that tender age. Thus, just before the war in Europe came to an end, I was enrolled in a sea catering training school in Myrtle Street, Liverpool, called Dicky Bond's, for a four week course, in order to become a Catering Boy aboard British merchant ships.

1

As Green as the Irish Sea

I was born and raised in the slums of an industrial town in north-west England, the youngest child of a family of six; with a Catholic mother of Irish descent and a Protestant father who I feel sure had Scottish antecedents.

One of my earliest memories is of lying in bed early in the morning and listening to clattering clogs of the mill-girls hurrying to their labours in the spinning mills which stood at the top of our street.

I received elementary schooling at St Marks, an Anglican Church school where there was much singing and religious instruction, but not much in the way of real academic education. There was no foreign language teaching, no science subjects, political economy or politics in general in the curriculum. I gained an ability to write in a legible hand and some knowledge of English grammar as well as a slight understanding of arithmetic.

My school-days were not a happy period in my life mostly because corporal punishment was in vogue at that time and was frequently handed out by both male and female teachers. However, I still felt a pang of regret when I reached the age of fourteen years and was told that I had to leave and seek my living with the rest of the working class.

During the next three years I had four jobs, firstly as an apprentice motor mechanic – which only lasted four weeks because I had a flaming row with the boss and left.

I then became a warehouse boy in a tannery for a year or so, when I left to work in the bottle-store of a brewery, where I developed an appetite for malt beverages. Eventually I received the sack for taking two weeks off in order to gain sea experience in one of His Majesty's minesweepers.

It was then that I got the most interesting job I have ever had: I became a groundsman on a 13-acre sports ground belonging to a famous textile firm. I feel sure that I would have stayed in this occupation for a long time but for the Conscription Act, so I decided to become a Merchant seaman. This was a Reserved Occupation and not liable to call-up to the armed forces at that time.

Sadly I left and took up a seaman's life. If anyone had told me then that it would be my calling for forty-two years I would have thought them candidates for the 'happy farm'. The training at Dicky Bond's catering school in Liverpool was composed of learning to make a sea-bed, lay up and wait at table, polish brass-work and training in how to handle a life-boat.

After four weeks we were passed out as catering boys and ordered to report to the Merchant Navy Reserve Pool on Mariners Parade in downtown Liverpool, where we were issued with a Discharge Book and an Identity Card – which contained a full set of finger-prints! We were also enrolled in the National Union of Seamen, at a fee of five shillings. When one Union official jokingly remarked that we had now become part of a million-pound organisation I never dreamed how much it would affect my life in the years to come.

Having passed out of the sea-training school successfully I was told to report to the Merchant Navy Reserve Pool where I was directed to join one of Shaw Savill's liners called *Akaroa* in Gladstone Dock, Liverpool.

She was a refrigerated cargo ship of some 11,000 tons net, with accommodation for 240 passengers and a crew of 120. I believe she was launched as *Euripedes* during the First World War, for the Aberdeen White Star Line, and saw service at the Gallipoli landings.

She seemed to have led a charmed life during the Second World War, because her triple propellers only gave her a speed of 14 knots in fair weather and I feel sure she must have been sighted many times by German U-boats during the Battle of the Atlantic.

Nevertheless, here she was towards the end of the war, loading general cargo for New Zealand via the Panama Canal and a full refrigerated cargo of meat and dairy products ensured for the 12,000-mile run home via Fremantle, Western Australia, Aden and the Suez Canal.

I must admit that the living quarters came as something of a shock, with the catering department billeted in 'glory holes' built into the stern end of the ship. With eight or ten men in each one of these not-too-large cabins, these were fitted out with iron bunks and steel lockers which vibrated furiously when the three screws started to rotate.

The deck and engine departments were not too much better off living in the forecastle with the consequent risk of being washed out, whenever the ship ran into heavy weather.

The voyage began on a bright sunny morning about 11 am when we were taken by four tug-boats from Gladstone Dock and anchored in the middle of the River Mersey to await the arrival of 240 passengers, who were to embark by tender in the afternoon with the two tenders shuttling between the ship and Liverpool Landing Stage until they were all aboard. We then lay at anchor awaiting the next high water, all night, and finally slipped away stemming the tide in the early hours.

I awoke about 4.30 am feeling somewhat queasy and realised that I was not going to be a good sailor. The ship was only pitching to a slight swell and here I was, already vomiting in the scuppers of the after well deck. Like Horatio Nelson, *mal de mer* was to be a chronic complaint during my life at sea.

The crew was a mixed one in the full sense of the word. There were mostly Welsh on deck, Londoners in the engine room, and the majority of the catering department was from Liverpool, with a fair number of Midlanders to complete the mixture. One of the latter was my best buddy, a lad from Coventry by the name of Patrick George Murphy. He was a handsome well-developed lad about five feet nine inches tall with a shock of brown hair and a suave and intelligent manner. There were also two lads from Preston, who completed the team of four Bell-Boys in the vessel. They had already been away to sea, but Paddy and I were as green as the Irish Sea and not allowed to forget it.

3

My Lancashire accent came in for much comment, and I at once started to adopt a Scouse one, which again caused much amusement among the Liverpudlians.

Fortunately the weather in the Atlantic was kind to us and we reached Caracas Bay in Curacao after 11 days of steady progress to take on oil bunkers enough to see us across the Pacific to our destination of Auckland, New Zealand.

Three days after leaving the Dutch Antilles we arrived at the Panama Canal and the port of Colon. We were scheduled to remain here overnight before starting the transit of the Canal on the following morning at 7 am. It came as a shock to hear that there was no money to be issued to the crew for the night ashore and this culminated in the entire Catering Department going on strike. Faced with the militancy of the stewards, the Old Man caved in and issued $10 (US) to the adult ratings and $5 (US) to the boys. Consequently a good night was enjoyed by all hands and I discovered that Yankee beer was capable of giving one a vicious hangover.

The transit of the Canal the next day passed without incident and one could not but marvel at the magnificent feats of engineering which must have been involved in the construction of this unique waterway, enabling a laden ship of some 24,000 tons to be raised 80 feet above sea level and then lowered again into the Pacific Ocean on the other side of the isthmus!

We completed the passage in 12 hours and stopped at the port of Balboa only to pick up some fresh vegetables and the few crew members who had missed the ship in Colon!

Now we began the 19 days haul across the Pacific to the Antipodes, stopping only for a few hours off Pitcairn Island to drop some mail and stores for the descendants of the mutineer Fletcher Christian and his crew.

The islanders, about forty in number, came out to the ship in their long-boats in a sizeable swell, to barter fresh fruit and wooden carvings for anything which was on offer from the passengers and crew. I was intrigued by the fact that they spoke Elizabethan English. It was an emotional moment when they returned to their lonely home, singing hymns such as 'We shall meet on that beautiful shore'.

4

Eleven days later we arrived in Auckland, described by some-body as the 'Pearl of the Pacific'. What I found most remarkable about it was that all the bars closed at 6 pm! The consequent rush of drinkers to consume as much booze as possible between 5 pm and closing time really had to be seen to be believed. It became known as the 'Six-o-clock Swill' and was a big question mark on the credibility of a so-called civilised country.

I never knew the reason for this state of affairs but I do know that it provided the opportunity for certain unscrupulous entrepreneurs to make some big profits from the operation of 'Sly Grog Shops' all over Australia and New Zealand which were patronised by Merchant seamen and Wharfies in every port in Australasia. Naturally the drink prices were inflated and the booze was watered – in order to achieve maximum profit.

We worked a 10-hour day, seven days a week for the total sum of £10 a month, which was made up of £5 wages and £5 War Risk Money, plus of course food and keep. An adult rating such as an assistant/steward received the princely sum of £23 for a 30-day month, £13 of which was wages. One can see that we could never be described as grossly overpaid.

The ship had been fumigated with cyanide gas just before leaving Liverpool but the bugs and cockroaches were active again as soon as we reached the Tropics. I never actually saw a rat aboard, but was told that they had developed a fur coat as a consequence of living in the fridge hatches. As regards food, we in the Catering Department didn't fare too bad because we dined on what was left after the passengers and officers had eaten. Many of the waiters and public room stewards made deals with the Chief Pantryman to get better meals than those of us who had no opportunity to make gratuities.

The Deck and Engine crew did not eat very well from their own galley up in the forward end of the vessel and there was many a visit by irate Able Seamen and Greasers to see Old Cresswell the Chief Steward and complain vociferously about the indifferent victuals being served to them. This situation did not improve until we arrived in New Zealand when the catering men also went on Crew Bill of Fare which culminated in an almost complete 'Walk Off' by all three departments in the port of Wellington.

By this time we were about two months into the voyage and many ratings decided they had had enough of British maritime life and decided to desert the vessel. This became so popular in Auckland that a detective called Dicky Bird was employed full time apprehending 'Ship Jumpers' who, when caught, were invariably fined a nominal sum or given a month in Mount Eden Jail, and then allowed to reside permanently in the country! These desertions reached such proportions that eventually in 1949 the British shipowners exerted some of their political clout and prevailed on New Zealand's government to pass into law a Deportation Act against foreign and British ship deserters. A large number of British seamen found work in New Zealand ships and in fact were instrumental in building strong maritime unions in Australasia – something they had been unable to do in Britain.

Eventually we completed loading our homeward cargo and sailed from Wellington in November 1945 hoping to be home for Christmas or the New Year.

We did not get off to a good start with a south-westerly gale in the Tasman Sea and the consequent five days of very heavy weather in the Great Australian Bight. Everybody was glad to see Fremantle heave over the horizon and wasted no time installing themselves in the pubs which were adjacent to the waterfront. The day ended with the Deck crowd being pursued back to the ship by a large hostile mob of Aussies intent on inflicting maximum damage on the Pommie sailors. The rest of the voyage was uneventful and quite restful.

2

The First Mistake

After two weeks leave I reported back to Liverpool Maritime Navy Reserve Pool and was directed to a ship belonging to Royal Mail Lines called *Durango*. She was employed on the South American frozen meat trade, carrying general cargo on the outward passage. It was supposed to be a voyage of eight or nine weeks but it actually lasted four months.

The crew was mostly from Liverpool with a sprinkling of outsiders or 'Woolly Backs' as the Scouser describes any non-Liverpudlian. We left the UK in good weather and five days later we bunkered at Las Palmas in the Spanish Canary Islands, which was a Duty Free port. Cigarettes and liquor were very cheap and could be sold in Argentina for a good profit.

The ship had fair weather and a good 16-knot cruising speed, so twelve days later we were in the River Plate and eagerly looking forward to a pleasant sojourn in Buenos Aires. The exchange rate was 12 pesos to the pound sterling, and a two-litre bottle of Quilmes beer cost only 80 centavos. I don't think there were any brothels as such but there were young ladies in most of the bars who, for a certain price, would take you to their rooms for a certain time of dalliance. This was before the president's wife Eva Peron got into her stride and had a vice crusade, successfully employing the girls on programmes of rehabilitation – much to the chagrin of the seamen, who looked forward to a 'run-ashore' in the 'Big Apple' as Buenos Aires came to be known to British seamen.

It took about 10 days to discharge our general cargo, and when the ship was empty we received the shocking news that, owing to the prolonged strike of the meat workers in the frigorificos, the ship was ordered to sail 'light ship' to New Zealand via the Straits of Magellan. This would put another three months on the trip! The passage began in a very pleasant and picturesque manner with us gliding through the calm Magellan Straits at the southern tip of South America and marvelling at the massive blue glaciers moving ponderously towards the sea.

We never imagined what awaited us at the Pacific end of the waterway. I had never seen such hillsides of water that hurled themselves at the Chilean coast and our bows. The ship was 'hogbacking' so violently in these massive waves that the wireless aerial which stretched from the centre-castle to the ship's funnel broke from its fixings and clattered on to the deck! Thus began a seventeen day passage which I remembered for years as the most miserable period of my sea-life.

When we arrived in Wellington, a great deal of work was needed on the hatches to ready them for loading a full cargo of lamb and dairy products (plus a large consignment of apples) in the port of Napier in Hawkes Bay. We had a quite pleasant stay of some four weeks, so much so that many of the crew decided to desert and stay ashore.

The one desertion I remember with much amusement was that of the Second-Cook and Baker, nicknamed Tab-Nab Tim by the Greasers, and who had not had a happy trip so far. The Chief Steward had pressured him about his sketchy knowledge of confectionery, and Bert, the ex-navy Chief Cook, had accused him of not pulling his weight in the galley. So on sailing night he had decided to 'skin out' and sell his labour power to a local bakery.

Half-an-hour before final departure the Greasers obligingly lowered him overside into a skiff, tied up under the wharf and there he sat with his suitcase, puffing away at his pipe, while the ship slid by on her way to the UK. Next morning when the ship was about 100 miles north-east of East Cape, the Chief Steward was hauled out of his bunk by the Cook and informed that the Baker had done a runner and that he, the Cook, had no knowledge of bread making. So here we were with three quarters of a crew, plus 24 fare-paying passengers and no Baker!

Captain Osborne was informed of the facts, and discovered that the Assistant Cook, one Percy Yegles, was the only person aboard who knew how to make bread. This was unfortunate for the Captain because he and Percy had crossed swords due to the fact that Percy and his mate, Conny O'Keefe, (one of the Engineer's stewards) had been 'logged' and fined heavily in Buenos Aires for returning late on board after their all-night carousing. Percy now had the whip-hand and extracted a hefty price for his agreement to be promoted to Second Cook and Baker.

First, he demanded that the loggings and fines he and his buddy had incurred be erased from the Log-Book, that he receive four hours overtime for each batch of bread he baked, and that I be rated up to Assistant Cook, which really made my day.

Apart from a rash of under-arm boils which were lanced regularly by the 'quack', and the many cut fingers I sustained in my efforts to master the art of using the big French knives when preparing vegetables, the homeward voyage was without incident.

On returning to the 'Pool after a couple of weeks leave, I made the first mistake of my sea life: instead of retaining the rating of Assistant Cook I allowed myself to be sent to an old Blue Star boat named *Fresno Star* as Engineer's Steward.

The ship was bound for Argentina – light ship (apart from extra coal bunkers which allowed her to complete the outward passage without bunkering and just a short stop at Madeira for fresh water). It took us 21 days to reach Buenos Aires where they immediately began to prepare the hatches for a full load of frozen meat and tinned corned beef to be loaded at Borisso near the city of La Plata. Again it was nearly a full crew of Scousers, but with the difference that the entire 'down below' crowd were of African and West Indian descent from Parliament Street in Liverpool 8. These firemen had done very well to steam the ship 6,000 miles in three weeks, but that was on good Welsh steam coal and it was a far different story on the long haul homeward on 'Yankee Slack'.

But I am getting ahead of myself and forgetting to describe my functions aboard this coal-burning fridge-ship belonging to Lord Vestey which had been a good earner in her long life.

I was the one and only Engineer's Steward aboard and I am certain that I had the hardest job in the Catering Department. There were ten engineers, each with his own cabin, plus the Radio Operator with his cabin, and a messroom which was not used for meals, only 'smokoes', but which still had to be kept clean by me. In addition there were two sets of bathrooms and toilets and I was delegated to do the 'strap up' in the centre-castle pantry at lunch and dinner times. To add insult to injury, every third day I had to get a tea-tray ready and deliver it to the 'Old Man' at a quarter-to-four in the afternoon. It can be seen that I had no time to stand around day-dreaming on this rustbucket and one can imagine how bitter and twisted I felt when I was presented with my account of wages in London by Mr Joe Burns, (Chief Steward) and discovered to my chagrin that he had paid me only 21 hours overtime during a two months and nineteen days voyage!

What a voyage it was thinking back on it; she bunkered three times during the voyage home; in Montevideo, Rio de Janiero, and St. Vincent in the Cape Verde Islands. The coal she loaded each time was 'Yankee Slack' – a very powdery type of fuel which meant the ship was covered entirely by a thick layer of it on each occasion. It was murder for the deck crowd to get the ship cleaned up again after bunkering, but at least they were paid plenty of overtime for their hard labour, unlike the Catering Department for whom it was all in a day's work.

I found out years later the reason why catering staff in Blue Star boats did not get paid overtime. It seems that the Catering Superintendent got his job from Lord Vestey on the understanding that he would cut the overtime bill of the Stewards Department by 80 per cent! His name was Hodkinson, alias 'Old Hodgie' as he became known – due to the fact that he introduced his son into the company and who eventually took over his job and became known as 'Young Hodgie'. He was not much of an improvement on his sire. I realised then that this kind of cheating by employers could only continue while we had a 'bosses union,' i.e. one that was completely subservient to the shipowners, and, in fact, was their lackey.

By then I had been at sea long enough to realise the deep and bitter hatred that seamen had towards this excuse for a union. It was much stronger even than the dislike they felt towards 'Company Men' who were the men who had sold their souls for a

Company contract. Little did I realise then, in 1946, that within twelve months the shipowners, in collusion with the so-called Union, would introduce the Established Service Scheme. This would force large numbers of seamen into signing a two-year contract which, for a pittance paid weekly while they were unemployed would result in direction of labour plus Disciplinary Committees with the powers to suspend or expel seamen from the industry for indiscipline aboard, or refusing to join certain ships. It was the worst thing that happened to seamen in peacetime.

3

State of the Union

The Establishment Scheme was certainly worth its weight in gold to the British shipowners. Considering the few quid they paid out in attendance money, they were given full control of the supply of labour, and the final say as to who would or would not work in the shipping industry. The National Union of Seamen were supposed to be the other side of what was called a Joint Supply System: but in reality they were only a rubber stamp in order to give respectability to any perpetrations the employers wished to commit on the seamen. How different it was for the stevedores and dockers who were safely ensconced in a government-controlled Dock Labour Board Scheme.

The Government was prepared to allow the seamen to operate under the same Reserve Pool they had enjoyed during the war, but our Judas representatives in the NUS stepped in and informed the Government that their members were quite willing to accept the shipowners' phony hiring and firing system. They even went to the trouble of organising a Special General Meeting of members in order to give credence to their servile support for the establishment of this blatantly illegal contract to be foisted on the seamen. But they made sure that the seamen who attended were faithful stooges of the Union and the Special Resolution for acceptance of the Established Service Scheme was passed into the policy of this iniquitous organisation. I described the Agreement as illegal with just cause, due to the fact that one of the first clauses in the pre-amble stated that the Owners were only prepared to accept 75 per cent of the labour force into the Scheme – regardless of the fact we were all members of the same Union, indeed forced to be, under the PC5 System. This was the closed-shop system which was given to the NUS by the shipowners in the 1920s when they realised that 'Toe Rag' Havelock Wilson, president of the union at the time, was more than amenable to their interests. This infamous one time Lib/Lab member of Parliament fought much harder against his members than any other union leader in living memory.

It is a very sad reflection on the British Trade Union and Labour Movement that this perversion of a labour organisation was allowed to be a member of the Trade Union Congress for so many years. Admittedly the NUS was expelled on two occasions from that body, once for forming a Scab Miners Union during the General Strike of 1926 and again in the 1960s for retaining the closed-shop system against the policy of the TUC. After each expulsion it managed to wheedle its way back in, and during the time it was expelled, no other union made any effort to poach its members, although they were entitled to do so under the Bridlington Agreement. The Transport and General Workers Union even had a seamen's section within it, but still made no effort to consign this Bosses Union to the dustbin of history where it so rightly belonged. To me, something was uncommonly smelly in Congress House, to allow this state of affairs to exist.

The reprehensible Established Service Scheme had only been operating for a few months but aroused such bitterness among the rank and file of seamen, that a strike broke out in the autumn. I don't know a lot about how it actually began, because I was away at sea when it happened, but I do know that the leader was a Scouse named Billy Hart, who was also a well known member of the British Communist Party. Consequently the strike was doomed to failure – firstly because the employers and the union played the 'Red Card' for all it was worth, and it has to be admitted that there was a large element among British seamen who were violently anti-communist and were not averse to scabbing. Secondly and more importantly the 'Comical Party', as I came to call it in years to come, was convinced to its Stalinist roots, that the National Union of Seamen was capable of being reformed into a democratic champion of the sea-faring proletariat. So the Party was not too happy about the feeling among the Scouses that it was

13

time to start building a new seamen's organisation and leave this so-called Union to stew in its own filth! This was tantamount to Trotskyist heresy as far as the King Street Commissars were concerned, and Comrade Hart was prevailed upon to come to an agreement with Tom Yates, the NUS General Secretary, that the *Queen Mary* would be allowed to sail, and the grievances of the strikers would be considered.

Thus it was that the first unofficial strike of seamen for many years was broken by the combined efforts of the Shipping Federation, the British Press and the National Union of Seamen. Within a short space of time, Billy Hart and Barney Flynn, along with other ringleaders, were arraigned at Liverpool Quarter Sessions, on a charge of incarcerating scabs during the dispute. Hart got six months in jail along with some of the others. They were also expelled from the shipping industry for life!

Billy tried to make a living on Panamanian ships but gave it up as a bad job eventually and came ashore to work as a scaffolder and rigger on construction sites. Here he made a name for himself in many bitter disputes, and finished up, I think, as President of the Constructional Engineering Union. It is a surprising fact that many of the militant seamen who came to the fore in unofficial maritime strikes, finished up in high positions in other unions after being flung out of the Mercantile Marine as *persona non grata* by the shipowners with the willing compliance of their vile lackeys in the NUS. In fact Tom Yates, who was later knighted for his services to shipping, actually advocated that young disaffected seamen on strike in 1955 should be called up into the Armed Forces.

Now in late 1947 the Owners had achieved success in their nefarious strategy to operate with a completely divided labour force. This consisted of four different categories: company contract men; established men on two year contracts with the Shipping Federation; Unestablished seamen who received no money for reporting to the Pool, and were only given employment after all the Established men had been directed to ships; and 'Appendix A' ratings.

The latter included bakers, laundrymen, printers, hairdressers, shopkeepers and other miscellaneous tradesmen considered to be completely outside the Established Service Scheme. This most evil and discriminatory hiring system went on for a long time because anyone who became discontented with it was soon dispensed with under the disciplinary procedures.

It became my lot to suffer this traumatic experience in the mid 1950s when I was serving as Assistant Ships Cook in a Shaw Savill line vessel called *Southern Cross*. Just after we sailed from Southampton on our round-the-world itinerary, we discovered that the Union had agreed with the shipowners that the overtime rate for the Catering Department should be cut by a shilling per hour from 2/6 to 1/6; this was greeted by much consternation by the cooks and stewards. I had the temerity to suggest that we form a shipboard committee to draft a 'Round Robin' which would be signed by all hands to inform the General Secretary that unless he went back to the Owners and restored our overtime rate we would be considering industrial action in the near future. I personally posted this missive to Maritime House in Clapham Common from Suva in Fiji by registered mail, as Ship's Convenor.

Captain Sir David Aitchison, commander of *Southern Cross*, was under the mistaken impression that I was operating as official Convenor, under the orders of the union, because when a handful of drunken hotheaded Scouses led a 'Walk Off' in Melbourne I was the guy who went on the quay and persuaded them that we were doing things the right way through the petition that we had sent to Yates.

In the next port, Fremantle, I made the silly mistake of returning to the ship twenty minutes after shore leave had ended, according to the sailing board. For this crime I was duly logged next morning and fined a nominal 10/- along with a whole bunch of defaulters. What really settled my fate though was the fact that a Canadian Party member called Saul Geller had taken it upon himself to send me a whole parcel of the Party publication, *Seaman's Voice* edited by an ex-Comintern agent named James Cameron – a real Scottish Stalinist.

This package had been opened by the powers that be up topside, who had at last realised that they had a real live subversive in their net. Remember that this was in the 1950s and the Cold War was raging on all fronts! The outcome was predictable; on arrival in Southampton, on the basis of the ten shilling fine, the Shipping

Master (a supposedly impartial Civil Servant of the Ministry of Transport) was prevailed upon by the Master to give me a Double DR in my discharge book.

4

Back on Dry Land

A 'Double DR' was known in the milieu as a bad discharge and not connected to the discharge one experienced after catching Ladies Fever! After receiving this bad report, seamen were required to face a committee in the Pool, composed of the Pool manager and the local union secretary – in this case a real 'no mark' called Bill Bryden. The minutes of the committee, which lasted all of fifteen minutes, were sent up to the Head Office of the Shipping Federation and the result that was sent back was a foregone conclusion. The Federation were not prepared to allow me to use the facilities of the Pool for the foreseeable future and I was to all intents and purposes blacklisted from the shipping industry!

The only thing the Party could suggest was to send me up to see a Party lawyer called Sedley of Sieffert & Sedley with modest offices in Holborn. This venerable old lawyer didn't seem unduly concerned about the fact that I had been unjustly restrained from following my trade but informed me that it would cost me £80 to get the case into the first Court and with not much chance of success.

I suppose that the Commos could be excused their uninterested attitude towards my predicament: after all, I had never accepted their many offers to take up membership of the British Communist Party. Knowing them as I do now, I was probably viewed with a degree of suspicion of being one of their *bêtes noirs*, a Trotskyite. All I was, actually, was a very naive radical seaman, whose only desire was to have an independent and militant union that would stand up and fight for seamen.

I had begun my association with the maritime communists some twelve months previously when I attended a seamen's rank and file meeting at the Town Hall in Canning Town, East London. This was at the invitation of another Canadian communist called Eddie O'Donnell from Iroquois Falls, Ontario.

There was a whole bunch of Canuck seamen in London at that period since the Canadian Seamen's Union had just been smashed by the Canadian government of Premier Louis St. Laurent, at the behest of the Canadian shipowners. I heard that he used the Canadian Navigation Acts which were even more draconian than the British Merchant Shipping Acts. He then allowed a union gangster called Hal Banks to enter Canada with the sole purpose of forming a 'Fink Union'. Consequently the militants of the CSU decided to try their luck on British ships, shipping out of the Port of London. However, they were soon weeded out when their records began to arrive from the Shipping Federation of Canada to their British counterparts.

This seemed to be the prime function of the International Shipping Federation – to keep tabs on militant seamen wherever they showed their heads. I don't believe that any other class of employee was kept under so much surveillance than that applied to seafarers. I'm convinced that at one time in the 1950s and 1960s, I was included in at least five separate agencies' filing systems. I know for certain that the NUS had a full dossier on me.

When we arrived at the meeting with comrade James Cameron in the chair, I was surprised to see a number of NUS officials in the body of the hall, one of whom was a virulent anti-communist called Ronnie Spruhan who reached the position of Assistant General Secretary of the NUS in later years.

The London District Secretary of the Union, Albert Butcher, was loitering in the foyer of the Town Hall, keeping a watching brief on the proceedings, and it seemed to be the intention of the officials to disrupt the meeting. But they reckoned without the militant Canadians who seemed very adept at countering this kind of interference.

This meeting began my long association with the editor and distributor of the *Seaman's Voice* Jimmy (Jock) Cameron, who I discovered was an international ex-organiser for the Red

18

International Trade Union Movement, and had operated in both the USA and Canada. He was also a veteran of the International Brigade which fought in the Spanish Civil War on the side of the Republican government. He had served in British ships in the engine room for a few years, but had retired with an injury to his spine. He was now operating on behalf of the Party as an organiser of British seamen. He used to try and sell the *Seaman's Voice* for a nominal sum to seamen drinking in various pubs around the Dockside districts in the Port of London.

What really got to me about the victimisation served out to me by the British shipowners was that I wasn't so egotistical to think that it was only happening to myself. I have no way of knowing just how many seamen got slung out of the shipping industry but I'm sure it must have reached sizeable proportions. Additionally, some of those who were expelled must have been men who went through the Battle of the Atlantic and were survivors of sinkings or who had spent many years in German and Japanese prisoner of war camps. One Canadian seaman was reputed to have survived being torpedoed on twelve separate ships at different times!

The contempt that the Owners felt towards their workforce was demonstrated even then in the middle of the Second World War . . . It is a little known fact, for example, that seamen's wages and allotment notes to their families were stopped from the time they were 'Discharged at Sea', i.e. lost their ship! A few years later these same heroes were losing their living because they had had the presumption to demand of their employers the wages and conditions they considered they were entitled to.

Their claim for better conditions came at a time when the Shipping Lines were making excellent profits as a consequence of a shortage of shipping (and the resultant high freight rates) which applied for quite a few years after the war in the liner and tanker markets. These exorbitant profits did not go to increase a seaman's wages because I know that ten years after the war, I was still on £23 per 30-day month – and have the Account of Wages to prove it.

To return to my predicament in 1956, I had to face up to the fact that after ten years at sea, with only a rudimentary knowledge of cooking and bread-making, there was the possibility of being ejected from the Seamen's Hostel – if and when they discovered that I was no longer a bona fide seafarer.

A Jewish lady by the name of Nancy Freed came to my aid by offering me a room in her four-roomed flat, which was situated in Wentworth Street – an extension of the famous Petticoat Lane and real Jack the Ripper country. It was also in the heart of the old Jewish ghetto near Toynbee Hall and a quite congenial situation.

The Party helped me to obtain membership of the Electrical Trades Union as an electrician's mate, and on that basis I procured employment on a 'carcase job,' a large block of offices being built in Gresham Street for an insurance company in the City. This was to be my occupation for a couple of years ... working on 'carcase jobs' until I had enough money to take me to Rotterdam to try my luck on the International Pool. Here I obtained work on Scandinavian and Dutch ships at infrequent intervals.

It was a sad existence and my hopes were still to get back into the old British rustbuckets ... although I must admit that the wages and conditions were better in the foreign flag ships. In the mid-1950s there was another unofficial seamen's strike. This time it was the young stewards in the Cunard liners who started the dispute, led by a youthful waiter called Les Hargreaves, if memory serves me correctly, and again it began in Liverpool!

This unofficial seamen's action in mid-1955 was a rather complicated affair, because the Stevedores and Dockers Union was in dispute at the same time. This was the 'Blue Union' which was supposed to be under the influence of the Troskyists, and in continual fratricidal strife with the 'White Union', i.e. the Transport and General Workers' Union which had a minority of communists on its Executive Committee. Whether the Trots had anyone liaising with the young seamen I don't know, but it was enough to send Jock Cameron post-haste to Liverpool to enlist the aid of his comrade Jack Coward – also an ex-International Brigader and a fellow Stalinist to boot. Again the reformist Party line was trotted out to the seamen; go back to work and try to reform this Shipowners' Union from within through Branch Meetings and Annual General Meetings. Comrade Coward set them an example by scabbing out on a 'Prince' boat from the port of Salford! Whether this dastardly action was on the orders of the Party Executive is open to conjecture, but years after the event, when I eventually heard about this misdeed, it certainly added to my reservations about the Comrades.

What really removed the scales from my political eyes though, was a visit to Moscow for an International Youth Festival in the summer of 1957 where we spent eighteen days as guests of the Soviet government. It was a marvellous experience and provided solutions to questions that I had been asking myself for years; such as, why did the Russians tolerate Stalinism and its evils for so long?

The answer to this question was glaringly obvious to me after only a few days in Moscow ... the Russian people were the most patriotic individuals in the world. I had by this time visited more than a few countries of the world but I had never experienced devotion such as these people showed towards their country. This explained why they rallied round the Red Flag when the Germans came over the borders of Mother Russia in 1941 ... they were not fighting for Uncle Josef Stalin but for their Motherland.

It very soon became apparent to me that this was far from being a Socialist State, with rampant discrimination between Party members and the ordinary Soviet citizens. The kids of Party members went to superior schools. There were special shops, selling luxury items which were in short supply – but only to card-carrying citizens – who for the most part could see nothing wrong in these class divisions. One of the most positive aspects of this society to me was the excellent language teaching system. I had never before met a foreigner who could speak faultless English without retaining a little of his native accent ... but it was commonplace to meet young Russians whose accents were those of the English Home Counties or American Mid-West!

5

James Callaghan and Other Encounters

When I returned to London from Moscow, I was asked my opinion of the Soviet Union by certain Party people, and I replied: 'With what they started with, and with what they have gone through the Russian people have done a marvellous job ... but I can't see that system lasting much longer!'

This heretical prognostication was not well received by the Comrades and from then I was viewed with suspicion. Nonetheless they were quite willing to accept my support at Union meetings where I became adept at chairmanship, not, I'm afraid, with the impartiality which is expected from that position.

My tutors in this had been Frank Chapple and Mark Young, two of the leading dissidents and ex-communists who had then gone on to conduct a battle within the Electrical Trades Union, and had been successful in toppling the Party leadership from their positions as President and General Secretary. I had warned Jim Cameron about this possible outcome of the irregularities which I had seen on my attendances at various ETU branch meetings. It seemed incredible that Party functionaries would emulate the same tricks and deceits that right-wing officials practised inside the National Union of Seamen. A Committee of Inquiry was set up by the TUC which concluded with the decision to expel the entire Union from the Congress, having accepted that there had been widespread and long-standing ballot-rigging within the ETU. Consequently a right-wing clique was installed, and included many of the ex-communists who had started the original enquiries. Chapple eventually became President of the Union and

Mark Young became National Organiser. The former went on to become Lord Chapple when he was given a peerage by either Wilson or Callaghan.

James Callaghan was a careerist in the Labour Party, and one of the three MPs I had lobbied in the 1950s. This was on the subject of my expulsion from the Pool and consequent loss of my living at sea. I chose him, along with Bessie Braddock and Emmanuel Shinwell because they all represented seamen's constituencies and had connections with the seamen's Union in the past.

Bessie Braddock came out of the Chamber first, and I didn't have much hopes of her help in my case because I knew she was a Catholic right-winger, and a violent anti-communist. Her solution to seamen's ills in general was for them to take a more active part in the affairs of the National Union of Seamen ... but she did not bother to explain how this could be achieved by seamen who were thousands of miles away from the UK for ten months of each year. Shinwell refused point blank to meet us, stating that he would need the permission of the NUS to do so! Lastly Callaghan arrived in the Lobby, and my hopes slumped further because this ultra-smooth operator had all the endowments of a Tory politician. He asked me what he could do for me and I replied that it would be good if he could ask the Tory Minister of Transport why it was that British seamen should have to work in foreign vessels because of the victimisation by their Union in a cabal with the Owners.

His reply to this request was succinct and terse. He said in his unctuous West Country accent, 'I don't think that will do you much good Mr Taylor, and it certainly won't do me any good.' It did not become apparent to me what he meant until years later, when I realised that this career politico had a special relationship with the Trade Unions, and went on to destroy Harold Wilson's industrial relations policy with the ill-fated In Place of Strife agreement – just to show Union oligarchs how much he valued their political and financial support.

That is why I found it deliciously ironic when these same so-called working-class organisations demolished his Government and his political career after a rash of strikes in The Winter of Discontent of 1978/79.

These interviews at the Palace of Westminster robbed me of any faith in Parliamentary and Social Democracy that I may have had up to that time, and made me realise that if I was going to get back into British ships, it would only be by my own efforts and ingenuity.

The answer came to me as I was browsing among some past issues of the National Maritime Yearbooks – a compendium of all Agreements in force in British ships at that time. My eyes were drawn to the Established Service Scheme and I noted that the Appendix A system was still in operation. I checked this out and discovered that various companies employed bakers. I then set about getting some phoney references with the aid of a local baker and confectioner who also initiated me into the rudiments of confectionery. Having worked on various ships as second cook and baker, I passed the trade test easily. The test consisted of 'Working By' several of Manchester Liners' vessels in the port of Salford for a couple of weeks.

Eventually I was signed on *Manchester Shipper*, a well-found ship of some 10,000 tons net. She carried a crew of about 50 and had accommodation for a few passengers. So I found myself in November 1959, slipping down the Manchester Ship Canal, outward bound for the port of Miami and other east coast ports of the USA.

The weather in the North Atlantic was as one would expect in winter, cold and boisterous although there is no guarantee of fair weather whatever the season in this most malevolent of the world's oceans. I could always sense if a seaman had spent a lot of time on the Western Ocean, they always had a certain air of melancholy about them. It certainly is a most fearsome place, especially if the weather systems are against one, which they usually are. We were fortunate and made the coast of Florida in twelve days.

Miami Beach, which was our first port of call, was a congenial spot. This was before Fidel Castro had sent the majority of his dissidents and criminals over from Cuba, which I believe has changed the place radically with a consequent increase in drug crimes, mayhem and murder. We were there for a few days, then made our way up the east coast via various other big ports, until we arrived in the Port of New York. I had already had fond memories of this place from my days in the Cunard liners. I found it was still an agreeable town providing, of course, one had the loot to make it so, especially at the Market Diner, a real seaman's watering place, opposite Pier Ninety in Manhattan.

We returned to Manchester via Dublin and I received a good discharge in my brand new Discharge Book. I was under the impression that I would then take my accrued voyage leave, but was quickly informed that I was expected to work by the ship while she was in port.

It was then that I made another serious mistake and decided to quit the ship and Manchester Liners, and try my luck elsewhere in the industry. I think that I tried for a job with the Pacific Steam Navigation Company at that juncture and again I was forced to work by several of their ships, before being allowed to sail for the west coast of South America in *Salaverry*, a motor ship engaged in trade with Colombia, Ecuador, Peru and Chile.

The Chief Steward was an Anglo-Spaniard called Perez and had a nasty habit of spying on his staff by stationing himself over the Galley fanlight, from where he could see and hear all that was going on below. The old Scouse Chief Cook finally cured him of this peccadillo by sprinkling black pepper on the hot stove, which was a very distressing experience for the 'Dago', as the cook used to call him. Perez seemed to have the main function of shop-keeper, because as soon as the ship arrived on the west coast, he became engaged in selling Yardley toiletries to the native spivs who came aboard at every port – and there are a hell of a lot of ports between Colombia in the north and Chile in the south! Sometimes we visited as many as three or four ports in one day, and on many occasions I met him coming up from his shop in the shelter deck in the early hours with a roll of American dollars, just about big enough to choke a donkey!

I found this first trip to the west coast interesting to say the least because of the prolific bird life and the grandeur of the Andes cordillera, which was very much in evidence after we left Peru. Our terminal port was a sailor's dream, and all the good things about Valparaiso that I had heard over the years exceeded my wildest expectations. It seemed to be the only place in South America with a genuine liking for British seamen; and that was not just the *senoritas,* but even the *policia* seemed to be more genial and forgiving of drunken mariners and their eccentric behaviour than in other ports I had visited in South America. Maybe it had something to do with the fact that an Irishman named O'Higgins had founded the Chilean Navy and helped the Chileanos achieve their independence many years ago. That is why I was so sorry when I learned of the military *coup-d'état* which took place years after my visit, and the subsequent inhuman crimes inflicted on the working-class by the Pinochet regime!

In my opinion the toppled President Allende made one fatal mistake ... he neglected to give arms to the workers. Someone years ago coined the saying that 'South America can be likened to a mendicant sitting on a gold-mine' and witnessing the poverty and sheer degradation of the ordinary people in these various Republics, one could only conclude that something was radically wrong with a socio-economic system which caused such misery to so many of their citizens. I reserved my pity especially for those native Indians of Peru who had been given an even worse deal than the Mestizos of that country. It still seems obscene to me that humanity can find the ingenuity and treasure to invent inter-planetary travel while allowing two thirds of this world's population to be suffering from under-nourishment all their miserable lives.

Anyway we finished loading our cargo of onions in Valpo and began our slow journey homeward to Liverpool via most of the ports we had called at on the way out. When we got to Liverpool, we found yet again an unofficial seamen's dispute, with a bed-room steward by the name of Paddy Neary as Chairman of the recently formed 'Seamens Reform Movement'. This was to be the vehicle by which British seamen would at last receive honest representation, equitable wages and better conditions. If it hadn't been so tragic it would have been comical. Here we were again on the same old merry-go-round. It was obvious to me that the Comical Party had once again got their agents into the leadership right from the onset of the strike. This time it was an Able Seaman by the name of Roger Woods, and he stuck close to Neary all during the dispute and for many weeks after it had ended. I have no doubt that it was he who sold the Reformist line to Neary and was helped in his efforts by that stalwart of the Labour Party, John Prescott. What an unholy alliance that was, but they were unable to fully control the bold Paddy because during the strike he disobeyed a High Court injunction to desist from inciting seamen and was jailed for Contempt of Court in Brixton.

During this period I returned to London and resumed my association with Jim Cameron. He asked me to keep my eye on the London Strike Committee of the National Seamen's Reform Movement which was chaired by a brilliant young chap by the name of Johnny Golden from Downpatrick in Ulster. He was in my opinion the cleverest and most dedicated rank and filer I have ever met, but he wasn't clever enough to see through the mendacity of the Communist Party and joined up just after the 1960 strike ended. This was mainly on his admiration of the Commissar Cameron, whom he discovered had feet of clay and was not the upright revolutionary that John had thought he was during the struggle. Shortly afterwards he married a Jewish girl called Helen, moved out of the Mile End area and dropped all his maritime acquaintances. I believe that he eventually became a big wheel in the Social Services Department of Waltham Forest in North London!

6

The Man Who Pays the Piper

The 1960 unofficial seamen's dispute was something of a watershed in the affairs of seafarers, because unlike other contests with the shipowners, after which everyone had dispersed to the four corners of the earth, this time there was some continuity and communication between the various ports in the UK. There was also a number of strong personalities which emerged during the struggle. Men like John Appleby from North Shields, Jim Slater from South Shields, Joe Kenny and Roger Woods with Paddy Neary from Liverpool.

About this time a character had turned up from Oz calling himself Gordon Norris (a.k.a George Goodman, originally from Tyneside) who was an ex-Australian Communist Party member and now raring to go and build a real rank and file communist seamen's movement on British ships. I must say that he got off to a bad start because one of the first things he did was to scab out in a Royal Mail Line ship for the west coast of the USA during the 1960 strike.

It became very noticeable over the years how he always managed to get all the good jobs and was never out of work for any long periods. Big John McGill from Paisley often remarked that Big G, as Norris came to be known, had the best work record of any union activist he had ever known. I had never known such a devious personality at sea, but I later realised that he was a true product of the Communist Party and its ideology. He rapidly displaced Jim Cameron and came to share the leadership of seamen activists, within the Union, alongside Joe Kenny, who had joined

28

the Party and announced his conversion loudly with a half-page article in the Communist Party newspaper.

Jim Slater did not commit his allegiance to the Party but maintained his membership of the Labour Party. Just how much of a fanatical Labourite he really was did not become apparent until many years in the future when, with the efforts of his Party colleagues, he managed to beat Ronnie Spruhan in a national ballot for the general secretary's position in the National Union of Seamen. There was much good feeling amongst seamen at this result because we all felt that at last we had a honest man to represent our interests. Little did we realise that we had merely changed a zealous Freemason in the person of Hogarth, who had recently died of a heart attack, for a fervent Labour Party disciple, in the shape of Jim Slater.

Many seamen, myself included, expected that he would have a purge of at least some of the right-wing officials in the union. Instead of which, he did just the opposite and promoted some of those who had actively worked against him during the recent election! He also made it known that he intended to increase the salaries of all the officials to a realistic level. This *volte-face* quickly earned him the sobriquet on his native Tyneside of Slater the Traitor with a few nasty epithets thrown in for good measure. Strangely enough, there was no reaction from the Marxists against this surprising turn of events, which paid dividends for them in the near future since we saw the spectacle in London and Liverpool of the Party Boys being given preferential treatment on the Pool.

There were so many Communists on Port Line ships doing coastal voyages and Run Jobs that there was some talk about changing the name of the firm from Port Line to Red Star Line. These same comrades became known on the Liverpool Pool as The Untouchables; that is, they seemed to be able to get away with many drunken escapades aboard without inviting sanctions.

By this time the Communist Party had a faction on the Executive Council of the union of about six, plus a few fellow travellers. Nevertheless the ferry boat men still maintained their majority on the Council and consequently supported the right-wing officials at the top of the so-called seamen's union, so that nothing had changed much regarding wages and conditions. All

three departments worked more hours than any shore establishment, and the wages and overtime rates were much lower than
Dockers received. The Merchant Shipping Acts were still archaic
and vicious in their attitudes towards the lower-deck seamen, and
looked as though they would stay that way for the foreseeable
future.

I refer now to the period prior to the election of Slater when Bill
Hogarth, a fanatic Freemason, was in the commanding position of
General Secretary. In 1965 he convinced the EC to let him go to
the Owners, where he negotiated a few pounds a month on to the
monthly wages of the labour force in return for a sixteen hours
increase on the weekly hours of all Departments. This infamous
deal was accepted by the EC but caused a lot of agitation among
the rank and file, encouraged by certain comrades, and which culminated in a unofficial stoppage in London and Liverpool. This
was quickly defeated, much to the relief of the Commos who were
very unenthusiastic about the unofficial action. Those who did
take part in this abortive strike were forced to sign a document in
the various Pools which stated that they would not involve themselves in any unofficial disputes in the future, on pain of exclusion
from the shipping industry.

Norris and other Party seamen were forced to endorse this
embarrassing instrument and I think that it was this shipowners'
stratagem that made the Communists so decisive in their efforts to
bring about an official strike in the following year. Because amazing as it may seem, that is exactly what came to pass almost one
year later, when the 74th Annual General Meeting of the National
Union of Seamen took place at Worthing from Monday May 2nd,
to Friday 6th of May, 1966.

It promised to be an historic and stormy conclave, because it
would be necessary to endorse the Strike resolution passed by the
Executive Council on the 14th of April of that year when they had
finally rejected the shipowners' final offer. In addition to which,
there had been a strong rumour that there had been financial irregularities in regard to the Union funds, so we of the left-wing bloc,
some 24 out of a total of 62 ordinary member delegates, plus 30
officials in attendance with full voting rights, did not feel very
confident of success at this congress. To our astonishment, how-

ever, we had virtually no opposition from the right-wingers throughout the length of the conference! The Strike vote was taken on the afternoon of the first day and passed without a single dissenting voice being heard. I found it difficult to believe what I was witnessing; here was a completely right-wing organisation altering policy in a most radical fashion, in support of a strike which would cost the Union a loss of £355,603 and cause the 1966 expenditure to exceed income by £257,884. A strike which anyone with a modicum of common sense could realise was unwinnable.

The year before we had gained a 12 per cent increase on our basic wage and added 16 hours to the working week for most of that increase. Now we wanted to retain the increased wage and reduce the week to 40 hours. It was also completely in contravention of the Prices and Incomes policy being pursued by the Labour government at that time. Added to which was the fact that the shipowners had been given adequate time to re-adjust their shipping schedules in order to avoid congestion in the ports and thwart the strike action.

It really was a most astonishing five days, so that on Thursday morning, when it came to the discussion on the salaries of officials, the left-wingers were in such a complacent frame of mind as to allow Hogarth an almost easy run in his efforts to explain away past discrepancies in the finances of the Union; in fact the whole of the debate on the Financial Report became something of an anti-climax, with comrades Norris, Kenny and Coward all giving nebulous contributions to the discussion.

On May 16th 1966 the Seamen's Strike began, and I was elected chairman of the London Docks Branch Strike Committee; my term of office was to last for the next seven weeks, and proved to be the most stressful period in my life. Fortunately for me, I had a very competent treasurer called Len Jones, a most intelligent Party member and a person I found very easy to work alongside. In fact I came to realise that his was the most arduous task on the committee, because not only was he responsible for paying out large amounts of strike benefit, he was constantly besieged by indigent seamen asking for money for lodgings and meals. He solved this by negotiating with the Sidoli family, who ran a café in

Leman Street. They agreed to accept his meal tickets from seamen and settle the account with him at the end of each week. I believe that he had a similar arrangement with the various seamen's hostels in London. He certainly never received any thanks and appreciation for his magnificent efforts during the long, nerve-racking dispute, which dragged on inexorably week after week.

By the 19th of May the Union reported that 410 ships were tied up and 11,885 NUS members were in dispute. By the 1st of June, 689 ships were idle and 19,730 members were out of work. On the 17th of June the whole Executive Council of the union went to 10 Downing Street, where the Prime Minister arranged a face-to-face meeting with eleven representatives each of the union and the shipowners – with no useful result.

During the first fortnight of the dispute our local committee was faced with the problem of the *Baltic Sun*, which was on a regular run to Gdynia in Poland, and which had arrived at one of the Pool of London wharves alongside Tower Bridge. She was full of dairy produce and Polish bacon, and because the crew had opened the forrard hatches before she tied up, discharge of this cargo began immediately. The problem arose when the dockers refused to open the after hatches of the vessel in order to complete the unloading. They took the view that this would constitute strike-breaking, but agreed that it would be acceptable for a party of striking seamen to open the hatch covers. This split the unity of our committee, and it was only after much pressure from the Central Strike Committee in the shape of Ronnie Spruhan, that I was forced to go with six ABs down to the ship and open the remaining hatches. This episode displayed the difference in attitude towards our strike by the two dockers' unions: The militancy of the Stevedores and Dockers Union and the amenable attitude of the TGWU as shown in the Royal Docks throughout the seven weeks of the dispute.

I found out after the smoke had cleared that there had only been about three oil-tankers held up during the seven-week dispute. Also, the strike committee in the Royal Group of Docks in East London, led by Comrades Coward and Norris, were allowing ships that had been discharged of cargo to be moved by Riggers of the TGWU so that another ship could be moved to the inside berth and begin discharging cargo. All during the strike roll-on–roll-off ships were being moved on and off the berths by deck and engineer officers in the port of Felixstowe to stop congestion in the port. All this was taking place, while so-called left-wingers were in charge of the strike committees.

While the ordinary dock delegates had a seven-week holiday, the right-wing did not relinquish complete control of the strike to the militants. Ronnie Spruhan and the National Organiser, a guy called Alf Gibson, who had made a rapid rise through the ranks of officialdom, were on the Central Strike Committee. Gibson was certainly no *dummkopf*, and proved it later on, after leaving the Union and becoming Personnel Manager for the Silver Line. I believe that he did eventually attain the position of Director of Personnel in Canadian Pacific Ships.

It never surprised me as to how many ex-officials of this union became employees of shipping companies because that was where their loyalties lay in the first instance; they were accustomed to doing the owners' bidding. When one looks at the situation objectively, the shipowners literally owned the union lock, stock and barrel because of the unique way that the employers collected the members' contributions and forwarded them to the union head office! This was known as List System and involved the seamen signing a document when they signed the Articles of Agreement. This entitled the employer to stop a weekly sum of money, i.e. the union contribution, out of the seamen's wages and these were forwarded *en bloc* to Maritime House at the end of the voyage. I feel sure that this 'sweetheart arrangement' was copied by other unions and became what we now know as a 'check off system' today.

It has always been my contention that a union which adopts such an arrangement, is no longer an independent entity and I have always maintained that 'the man who pays the piper, calls the tune'.

It is said that this set-up was given to the infamous Havelock Wilson in conjunction with the PC5 system back in the 1920s because the employers knew full well that no seaman would have contributed to the NUS on a voluntary basis. Therefore the shipping companies introduced an element of coercion into their hiring system, and when this was challenged in the High Court by a Greaser named Collins, they won the case because the judge gave a mis-direction in his summing up. He maintained that the shipowners had a legal right as to who they employed and completely ignored the fact that they were acting illegally in their restraint of the man's trade by the adoption of this coercive instrument! Once having got the decision, it became Case Law and the employers were home and dry, along with their myrmidon Havelock Wilson.

Here we were forty years on and the Communist Party having been given a golden opportunity to destroy this unholy alliance which had battened on seamen since its inception, threw it away by dragging the British seamen into a prolonged futile dispute which we had no chance of winning. I must state to be fair that the ordinary rank and file members of the Communist Party gave us tremendous support, both financially and by donations of food to the strikers' families. In fact the dispute was still receiving rock solid solidarity from the seamen when the Communist Party in the persons of Jack Coward and Gordon Norris decided that enough damage had been done. Norris told the Executive Council: 'I'm afraid that we have reached the end of the road, Brothers.'

7

Union Sharks and Barracudas

This was the conclusion of the first official strike of the misnamed National Union of Seamen in its seventy years of existence and there was much bitterness amongst the members, many of whom realised that the strike was just beginning to bite when it was called off. Now the dock delegates could go back to their nefarious ways – one of which was going aboard ships before sailing to give warnings to the heads of department that there were some militants aboard, and furnish them with names. This meant that the union activists were targeted from the outset of the voyage. One of the officials who indulged in this practice was Bob Fleming in the Victoria Dock Branch who became known to the militants as 'The Poison Dwarf'. Another was the infamous Taffy Fabini from Dock Street Branch in London, who dealt mostly with the General Steam Navigation Company, a subsidiary of the mighty P&O Lines.

After the strike Steve Leek, a union activist, got a job in the *Swallow*, a Mediterranean trader belonging to GSNC as a 'skipper's tiger' or saloon steward. During the trip he got friendly with the third mate, who told him that the bold Fabini had informed the Old Man that Steve was a well-known agitator in the Union! Unfortunately Brother Leek was unable to persuade the third mate to put this *exposé* into writing.

During the voyage, Steve was 'logged' for swearing at the captain, and after refusing to give him a verbal apology for this misdemeanour, he received a double DR at the end of the voyage. Naturally, he blamed Fabini's exposure as the reason for the harsh treatment he had received and wrote to Hogarth, asking that the Welsh Wop be disciplined by the EC. Taffy got away with a castigation by Hogarth and told to watch his step in the future. The other official, Fleming, went on to canvassing the marine superintendents of various companies and asking for voyage reports on activists, as to whether they had indulged in homosexual adventures on board with the 'sea pussy' (as the American seamen called maritime sex deviants).

It was a great pity that The Poison Dwarf was not born in the Soviet Union: he would have had a great career in the KGB. I only found this out about Fleming when I mentioned to John McGill that a certain Communist militant had become quite muted and inactive recently. He told me that Fleming had discovered that the Comrade (who shall be nameless) had a predilection for young boys, and had forwarded the good news to Sam McCluskie and Jim Slater at 'Clap House'.

So here was another use for the voyage reports which were composed by the heads of department after every trip and were in addition to the Pool dossiers and the files kept by the union on anybody who became too vociferous and troublesome. Strangely enough it was Slater and Joe Kenny as lay members of the EC who had accompanied General Secretary Hogarth, and Gerry Lipman, Assistant General Secretary and Treasurer, on a fraternal visit to the Soviet Union, as guests of the Soviet Maritime Unions for a couple of weeks. So maybe 'Wor Jim' had learned a thing or two from the Moscow comrades during his brief sojourn in the USSR. He certainly retained a sense of loyalty to Kenny, because when years later Joe was diagnosed as having a liver cancer, Slater as General Secretary took it upon himself to appoint Joe to one of the top jobs in the NUS so that Joe's widow would have a decent pension when he died, as he then did, a couple of months later.

Sam McCluskie, who finished up as the last General Secretary of the seamen's union prior to its amalgamation with the National Union of Railwaymen, was a classic example of a seaman who saw the integral connection of the Labour Party and the seamen's union.

The relationship went back for a long time, and the officials were expected to canvass both locally and nationally for the party.

In fact Sammy eventually became Labour Party Treasurer and had a seat on the Party Executive for a long time. His party connections certainly caused him to climb rapidly through the union hierarchy in a few years. The time span from his beginning as a dock delegate in Grangemouth to a position in Head Office was less than ten years, and it was his proclivity for manipulating people which made him successful and gained him the top position at Maritime House. A strange thing about this political animal was that he never, to my knowledge, ever admitted where he stood on the political spectrum! To me though, his actions spoke louder than words.

When the TUC instructed all unions to renounce closed-shop agreements, it was 'Sam the Man' who visited all NUS branches to tell the membership that he did not see how the union could continue without the PC5 system being a part of the hiring set-up in the future.

In my opinion it was McCluskie who was mainly instrumental in permitting British shipowners to retain their source of cheap labour, in the shape of Asiatic crews from India, Pakistan, and Hong Kong later in 1982. He was also responsible for the implementation of the 'Asian Levy', in which large sums of money were paid by the owners to the union for the continuation of employing Asian crews. It worked out at £15 per Asian employed. The British shipowners saved about £50 million a year in crew costs by employing Asians and the levy made only a tiny dent in that figure.

Back in mid-1970, a joint working party of shipowners, the union and the Government produced a report on the employment of non-domiciled seamen. It rejected racial discrimination as immoral, but realised that raising wages all at once would cause social and economic problems. Its recommendations included staged payments up to 1982 which would bring Asian rates up to those of NUS members. This proposal was endorsed by the Government but was never implemented. Needless to say neither Slater or McCluskie did anything about it. So we had a situation at the end of 1982 whereby of the 26,000 registered British seamen, 2,000 were unemployed, thousands had been made unfit for seagoing and a few had been made redundant and paid off. There

37

was now only 18,000 jobs left, and 6,000 of them were taken by Asians.

I firmly believe that it was this act of treachery that caused Prime Minister James Callaghan to award Slater the high decoration of Commander of the British Empire as one of his last acts of preference when he bowed out of political life. It seems superfluous to state that trade union leaders do not receive such marks of distinction as a CBE for defending the interests of the hoi polloi – even if those same proles are furnishing you with a very congenial living with their weekly dues. My somewhat convoluted thinking leads me to believe that Callaghan's gratitude was a sign of his adherence to the ruling classes: ergo, whatever favoured his masters was commendable in his estimation. I realised where Lord Callaghan's fealties lay when I noted in the *Sunday Express* in 1955, that the obsequious MP for Cardiff North had been invited to a dinner party at Buckingham Palace. This caused me to remark to Jim Cameron that 'Oily Jim' was being groomed for stardom, another of my political hunches which came to pass.

Perhaps now is the time to end my political perambulations and return to 1947 when I was transferred to Avonmouth Pool and directed to join *Bayano* – my first experience of a 'skin boat' belonging to Elders & Fyffes Co which was, or became, a subsidiary of the United Fruit Company of New York. She was built for the carriage of bananas but had spent the war on the North Atlantic, bringing cargoes of bacon and eggs from Nova Scotia in Canada, and had accommodation for forty passengers. Now she was back on her peacetime run between Avonmouth and the banana ports of Jamaica and Trinidad. Although a coal-burner, she was scheduled to do the round voyage in four weeks because she carried only a small amount of general cargo on the outward passage. Also, the loading of the fruit in Jamaica continued round the clock when we arrived at the various ports, which if I remember correctly were, Bowden, Orrecabasa and Port Antonio. So the trip was split roughly into three parts of ten days outward, ten days on the coast and ten days for the homeward passage.

These ships did not seem too popular with seamen – and I very soon discovered why. When we encountered a Force 8 gale in the Western Approaches shortly after departure from the Bristol

Channel we spent a very uncomfortable three days, during which I realised that these banana boats were in no way sea-kindly, and had a very erratic motion in any kind of a seaway. The trouble was that they were light ship whether they were loaded or not, and although they went south of the Azores on the way out, on the way back they took the Great North Circle track, in order to keep the cargo from ripening, with the consequent risk of heavy weather.

It was told to me that a Colonial colonel on the way homewards had confronted Captain Gracie and asked him to slow the ship down in order to alleviate the motion because the memsahib was as green as grass. Captain Gracie was supposed to have told the Colonel that this was the same colour he intended to keep his cargo!

It must have been murder down below in the stokehold and coal bunkers in bad weather for the firemen and trimmers, particularly in view of their 'chicken-shit' wages of sixteen shillings a day plus bed and board of a very indifferent calibre. It was very near industrial peonage. The firemen and trimmers lived in the stern over the propellers, and if the weather was very bad, they had to go to and from their work place via the tunnel which housed the propeller shaft. It was little wonder that they went on the bottle when they got ashore in Jamaica. The maximum amount of cash issued to all hands was £5 per man which did not seem much, but with rum at five shillings a bottle, it enabled them to get in some awful states of intoxication with consequent fits of violence. It was a very good reason to go teetotal, and I realised why this lovely country of Jamaica had come to be known to British sea-men as 'crackers island'.

We dropped the passengers in Kingston and then moved over the bay to Port Royal to load coal bunkers for the homeward trip. This was when the bacchanals began and the captain very wisely gave a day off to all the crew. Away we all went in the ferry launch to Kingston Town where we proceeded to 'splice the mainbrace' with wild abandon. I discovered that a rum called Appleton's Estate mixed with Coca-Cola and ice to form a drink called Cuba Libre was very much to my taste. Unfortunately, nobody bothered to tell me of the horrific hangover which awaited me the following day!

In addition to feeling violently ill, there was also an experience of deep depression which lasted for the following two days. An old bedroom steward, seeing my distress, decided he would cheer me up by recounting the high numbers of seamen he had known on skin boats who had decided to put themselves over the side after departing from Jamaica. It was this fact that had earned it its nickname!

Strangely, on a later voyage in a sister ship called *Cavina* I was unlucky enough to witness the truth of his words. A chap called Bill Mitchell who was assistant head waiter and from Edinburgh, received a 'Dear John' letter when he arrived in Kingston. This was sufficient to send Billy on the bottle, and keep him on it all the time we were on the coast. The night we left Port Antonio for Avonmouth, Billy came round all the glory holes with a king-size bottle of rum, insisting that everyone should have a drink with him for *Auld Lang Syne* as he put it. The following morning, the night-watchman reported him missing to the officer of the watch.

The ship was turned about immediately and continued a search for four hours without sighting anything. The firemen told the Old Man that they had seen Billy standing on the after well deck, when they were coming off watch at 4 am, clad only in his underpants! His demise cast a pall of gloom over the ship and I could only hope that he drowned quickly, for the place where he disappeared, the Windward Passage, was the habitat of big sharks and ferocious barracudas.

Strange though it seems, I received a message from him some years afterwards, during a spiritualist meeting that I had been invited to by a lady friend. The medium told me that someone called Mac, who he described correctly, was telling me that I was one very lucky seaman.

8

On Becoming a Distressed British Subject

It was shortly after leaving *Cavina* that I had my first experience
of the Union Castle Line when I joined one of their Mail Liners
called *Warwick Castle* in the port of Southampton. She was a very
good-looking ship of some 20,000 tons with a couple of fridge
hatches, and luxurious accommodation for a few hundred passengers in two classes. I signed on as the officers' steward and looked
after the deck officers, comprising of the chief officer, first and
second, third and fourth officers plus two radio officers, so I had
seven cabins to clean and seven bunks to make, added to which
were two bathrooms and lavatories, a pantry and the alleyways in
the officers' accommodation to keep spotless. In addition I had to
wait at table in the First Class saloon, to serve the junior officers
and both 'Sparks' for three meals each day. There was also coffee
and tea to be served in the morning and afternoon plus tea and
toast on the bridge for the first officer just after 6 am every morning at sea. What really got up my nose was the chore of
serving the second officer rolls and marmalade with a jug of coffee
every morning at 9 am in bed, after he had done the 12 to 4 am
watch at sea.

The itinerary was Funchal, Madeira; then Capetown, East
London, Port Elizabeth, and the terminal port of Durban in Natal,
with the same ports on the way home. The voyage took six weeks
round trip on a service speed of 16 knots and she was as regular as
clockwork due to the Royal Mail contract which the company had
for South Africa.

I lived along with two engineer stewards and the 'skipper's

41

tiger' in a four-berth cabin on the Bridge Deck and good cabin mates they were; there was Boris Williams from Birkenhead, his mate Allan Gilmour from the Isle of Man who sad to say finished up in a pauper's grave in Liverpool, and the Tiger who hailed from West London and who always maintained that he felt like an alien amongst us three Northerners and our, to him, very quaint accents.

It was very congenial living with these companions, for the Tiger could always get hold of a bottle of spirits from one of the barmen, added to which we had our daily issue of three bottles of 'Cape Lager'. Then when we arrived at Capetown, we used to put equal amounts into the kitty and order large amounts of South African port wine, sherry, and Cape Brandy, which was duly delivered to our cabin by the liquor store salesman.

Unusually for me, I did two consecutive trips in this ship, and then, when I realised how much alcoholic liquor I was consuming, came the decision that discretion was the better part of valour and I abdicated gracefully afore I contracted Doctor Korkasov's Syndrome.

It was during this period in 1948 that the infamous Apartheid policy was introduced into South African politics, which came to mean the forcible separation of white and coloured races. What struck me as ironic about this was that many of the whites who were avid supporters of this regime were themselves carrying coloured blood in their veins. This was because miscegenation was an accepted fact for the first Dutch white settlers of the Cape Colony. It was a few years later before I realised just how much of a police state South Africa had become.

I was in a ship called *Good Hope Castle* which flew the South African flag and was registered in Cape Town. She had five hatches, with Jumbo derricks forward and aft for heavy lift jobs, and carried general cargo outwards to the Cape, Natal and Mozambiquean ports before loading bagged sugar in Port Louis in Mauritius and topping up in Mombasa with bagged coffee.

When we arrived in Cape Town on the way out from UK we agreed that the chief cook and the galley boy should finish work for the day, after lunch was over. Charlie the assistant cook and myself, as second cook and baker should take the following half-day off. This applied to all the time we were in port.

On the day we were due to sail for Port Elizabeth Charlie and I left the ship at 1.15 pm taking note of the sailing board, which said the vessel was due to depart at 7 pm and shore-leave ended at 6 pm. We had a pleasant afternoon visiting various hostelries and returned to the berth at 5.50 pm only to find it was empty, except for a very large member of the Cape Town Constabulary. He demanded our names and then offered to escort us to a place where we could get our heads down. This turned out to be the local immigration compound, and by 7 pm we were safely ensconced behind bars, along with other miscreants who had found themselves *persona non grata* with the authorities. One East German had been in the lock-up for a year while the South Africans canvassed the world, looking for a country which would accept the stateless deportee.

Next day Charlie and I were taken under guard to the train, and the 48-hour journey to Port Elizabeth began. It started in quite a convivial manner, with two Boer farmers in our compartment inviting us to share their bottles of Orange Gin and beer. It was a relaxed and pleasant way to travel, with good meals served to us at regular intervals.

The scenery was magnificent when we started to cross the mountains. Two days later we arrived back at the ship and Captain Fisher wasted no time in pronouncing the penalty for our folly. We were fined three days pay and forfeited three days pay in addition to our paying the train fare. One could only conclude that it had turned out to be a very expensive half-day off.

It was years later before I discovered that it was illegal under the Merchant Shipping Act of 1894 for a shipmaster to leave a seaman behind in a foreign port without the permission of a proper officer – such as a British consul or marine superintendent of the local shipping office. This kind of incident must have happened on hundreds of occasions but in all the years I spent at sea, I have never heard of a ship's captain being prosecuted and fined the £100 mandatory penalty.

One case that stays in my memory is that of a Greaser named Malone, who had been deported along with many other alien seamen from the USA in the 1950s, for their subversive tendencies. Malone was accused of being a Trotskyite agitator in Yankee ships he had served in during the Second World War. After this he was, along with other alien seamen, forcibly expatriated to the UK. The way he described it to me was that FBI agents seized him on board an American ship when he was paying-off, distrained his wages and escorted him to Pier Ninety in the port of New York where he was given a cabin in the *Queen Mary* in the tourist class accommodation and for which the requisite fare was deducted from his pay. The remainder of his cash was paid to him five days later on arrival in Southampton. I think Tom Blower, a Nottingham chap, was treated in the same way and finished up in the same Sailor's Home in Dock Street, London.

Tom had no belief in politics but was a pure anarchist whose solution to the ills of the capitalist system was the sub-machine gun which could fit into a waistcoat pocket. To the best of my knowledge, Tom never did make it onto British ships, but Malone, who was made of more devious stuff, contrived by some duplicity and guile to obtain false papers which enabled him to gain employment in British ships. However, on account of his abrasive attitude with the officers or 'gold braid' merchants on board, his British maritime career did not last more than a couple of trips. The end came when the captain of a Houlder Line ship sent him ashore to the dentist in Bahia Blanca, Argentina, when Malone complained of neuralgia.

Once Malone was in the dentist's chair, he was given a needle of narcotic and when he regained consciousness, his ship had departed for UK home and beauty ... so the comrade Malone came home as a Distressed British Subject on another ship with a big fat 'voyage not completed' in his 'Fink Book' as he liked to call the British Discharge Book.

His ejection from the Pool was rapid and decisive, and from then on he subsisted on shore donkeyman's jobs, which he acquired from a Rigging firm over in Bermondsey, on the basis of his wide experience in ships' engine rooms.

He was a sagacious person and it was he who pointed out how much the British shipowners were cheating their seamen, by paying them on the basis of a thirty days month! He calculated that the owners were gaining at least six days per man per annum and if that was multiplied by 65,000 men, it would pay a hell of a lot of bunkering charges and pilotage fees.

He maintained that the 'Limey shipowners' were running their ships on money rightfully due to the 'Working Stiffs'. Little wonder that the NUS delegates gave him a wide berth. The last I saw of him was in a Seamen's House in Gothenberg, Sweden; seemingly he had managed to get a motorman's job in a Swedish ferry which ran between Gothenberg and Tilbury.

Not content with the liberal wages he was getting on the Swede, he had decided to try his hand at smuggling watches into the UK and finished up 'getting his collar felt' in Petticoat Lane with a whole parcel of contraband on his person. He was fined about £60 at Thames Magistrates Court and sacked when the ferry got back to Sweden, so he was beached again.

But I have no doubt that he managed to ship out later because he was very astute and used to overcoming the usual mishaps of life at sea. I would have liked to hear the full story of his life.

9

Corruption

I think it might be politic at this stage to mention my short career with Cunard White Star Line. It began when I was directed to a troop-ship belonging to them, called *Georgic,* as a bathroom steward. She was about 20,000 tons and capable of carrying 6,000 service personnel. The war had not been kind to her because she was attacked in Suez Roads, near Port Tewfik at the southern end of the Suez Canal, by Italian bombers who had managed to land an oil bomb down her funnel, causing immense fire damage. Fortunately, it was possible to beach her and extinguish the fires. I think she was consequently towed away to Durban to be repaired and was successfully operated until the end of the war.

In 1946 when I joined, she was engaged in bringing the troops back home from the Far East, mainly India and Singapore. My function as a bathroom cleaner was not too arduous but I suffered badly from prickly heat rashes when we got east of Suez and down the Red Sea.

We dropped the main body of Army Cadet Officers in Bombay and then continued across the Indian Ocean to Singapore. The thing that sticks in my memory was the large amounts of Japanese occupation-era dollars blowing round the streets, now completely worthless. *Georgic* was an exceptionally warm ship and the experience of 6,000 service men and women being sea-sick, at the same time, in the Bay of Biscay in a Force 8 gale, was a salutary one. It convinced me to pay off and say farewell to good old *Georgic.*

When I returned to the Pool after my leave ended, I was drafted along with a couple of hundred more seamen to Southampton to join *Queen Mary* as engineers' steward.

She was undergoing a complete refit in the dry dock for her return to passenger service on the New York run, and the engineers and mates were being catered for on board during the long lay-up.

My job was composed of keeping the engineers' cabin clean and sometimes waiting on table in the cabin class saloon. I would have probably sailed in this ship but for the fact that I became involved in a vendetta with a plateman called Arthur Newby from Garston, a suburb of Liverpool.

When he told me where he hailed from, I made the mistake of saying in jest, 'Is that where all the Judies sit with their legs up on the piano in the pubs?'

He immediately took umbrage and from then on we were at daggers drawn! We got into the habit of joining battle when we returned from ashore and slightly under the influence of a few Boilermakers (brown ale and bitter mixed). The Master at Arms became so tired of separating us when we clashed on A deck foyer, that I was eventually transferred to the sister ship *Queen Elizabeth*. She was already back on her peacetime run of five days across to New York, with two days in that port and five days run to Southampton.

My job consisted of feeding two sittings of eight engineer officers in their dining room up on the boat deck. If memory serves me right there were eighty-nine of these creatures and they used to eat the same as fare-paying passengers; and with great gusto as if they had just been released from a Japanese prisoner of war camp after prolonged incarceration.

Whoever named these two ships *Queen Mary* and *Queen Elizabeth* certainly gave them the most appropriate titles because I had never seen so many homosexuals and their catamites in one ship at the same time – and it wasn't just the catering department. The 'limp wrist brigade' was recruited from all the strata of the crew which numbered about 1,200.

The Chief Engineer's Writer was a big Australian queen and he was the first one I had ever seen. In addition to having one of the best jobs in the *Lizzy*, he was also the number one bookmaker in the vessel and would offer odds on any wager; he was so affluent that he could afford to fly south when the ship was in New York, and attend race meetings in Kentucky and Florida.

I had no strong opinions about homosexuals during my time on this ship because I could not afford to since they were virtually running the show. But one aspect of their character which I really found obnoxious was their penchant for luring the heterosexuals into their perverted ways, and then publicising the fact that they had gained another convert.

This ship was the most well-to-do ship I ever worked in. Everyone always seemed to have plenty of mazuma. How they got it I don't know. It could have been smuggling or gambling, or the fact that there was an exorbitant amount of overtime to be made. The end result was that the 'Pig and Whistle' (both of them) were always full of parched seamen and the poker schools and crap games went on into the wee small hours at sea and in port.

I realise now that the Cunard practice of paying out the previous fortnight's overtime at regular intervals on board at sea was why there was so much cash swilling around the ship at all times.

In retrospect there was also the sizeable amounts of 'Dropsie' that the 'wingers' (waiters) and 'pisspot jerkers' (bedroom stewards) received from their 'bloods' or 'punters', as the passengers were known.

With all this lucre came corruption. Unscrupulous careerists would pay money to the second steward for a better job, and this would mean an increase in the amounts of gratuities for the miscreant. What really amazed me was the practice of anyone who had the money being able to order a food box, priced from £1, £5 to £10 according to how much you wanted. The initial request was made to one of the pantrymen, but there must have been all kinds of people involved in this larcenous racket. It was on such a grand scale that I'm convinced that the higher management was involved and responsible for turning a blind eye so that nobody, in all the years that it continued, was ever arrested and prosecuted for the swindle. God only knows just how much this fraudulent conspiracy cost Cunard Line, but it must be in the millions because I learned later it was customary in the Cunard liners.

How much money 'talked' on this ocean greyhound became

48

clear to me when I noticed one day, as I was signing for my over-time at the Writers Office, that opposite my name were the words 'Engineers' Pantryman'. I pointed out to the Writer that I was in fact a messroom steward, he replied, 'Oh yes, but you were rated-up to the higher rating a few weeks ago with a consequent increase in wages.'

When I confronted Jack Mott, the chief messroom steward, with the facts of my promotion, he went down post haste to Nichols, the ginger-haired second steward, who was a brother Freemason of his, and I was sacked and paid off the *Lizzy* within two hours! It was obvious to me that Mott the Mush had taken a back-hander for the job.

I wasn't sorry to be out of this virtueless vessel, and the fact was that at that time, in Liverpool, there was more ships than there were Parish Church steeples. Moreover life was much less com-plicated and onerous in cargo ships.

Years before in British ships, from what I heard from the old-arses, the Master stood the 8 to 12 watch on the bridge, with a mate to do 4 to 8 watch and a second mate to complete the 12-hours cycle on the 12 to 4 watch, plus three engineers to do the same in the engine room. There was also a wireless telegraphist and a chief steward. Most skippers would not allow engineers to dine in the Captain's saloon with him and the Mates, but insisted they eat in their Messroom. That was all the so-called after-guard consisted of until the Second World War, when British shipowners decided to change the Mercantile Marine into the Merchant Navy and emulate the Royal Navy. This was of course all part of the old divide-and-rule strategy which had been practised by the British Ruling Class from the days of the Roman occupation of Britain. The fact remains that none of these bogus officers was ever given a commission from the King, but they were indeed employees of the shipping industry, like the rest of us. So we had the ludicrous situation of a young Engineer Officer, whose previous job had been as a can-lad in a shipyard, coming aboard to do his first trip and ordering some hairy-arsed steward to scrub his cabin out, change his sheets and bring him a pot of tea in the mornings.

They even had their own better brands of soap and towels issued, along with white sheets and counter-panes – in contrast to the blue sheets and Army blankets which were reserved for the Scabby-Heads. We also saw cadets (or apprentices as they were called pre-war) coming aboard, with their brand new uniforms, as the rising generation of 'gold braid merchants'. In fact some of the shipping companies had purpose-built ships for these budding officers to train in which were employed on commercial voyages to the Antipodes.

I was in one cargo boat where the deck apprentice became friendly with the ship's deck-boy, and they were in the habit of going ashore together. The Old Man spotted the pair of them on the quay one Sunday afternoon in San Francisco and on their return he forbade them ever to go ashore again in the future!

This blatant class distinction, which became the norm in British ships, soured industrial relations and brought about an 'Us and Them' factor. I must admit that the deck crowd or some of them, seemed to hold a certain amount of respect for the deck officers, whereas the Ginger Beers as they came to be known, seemed to be held in contempt by all hands – especially by their stewards who had to clean up after them.

Another source of discord was the fact that all the engineers were entitled to regular issues of spirits such as whisky, gin or rum. So the situation could arise whereby a chief cook with long sea service could be refused a bottle, whilst a junior engineer would get one every week. This was a very sore point because the amount of Bonded stores such as cigs and tobacco, along with beer, wines and spirits that the Customs and Excise allowed on board, was based on the total number of crew members in the vessel.

Then there was the ludicrous situation whereby the saloon was fed on a breakfast, lunch and dinner system, while mess-room denizens received breakfast, dinner and tea! Even the petty officers such as the bosun, carpenter and engine-room storekeeper, or donkeyman, and possibly bosun's mate and carpenter's mate were served by the deck-boy or crew-messman in a separate messroom on the saloon Bill of Fare.

If the ship was a passenger liner there would also be a separate messroom for the three or four quartermasters, whose function was to keep the Bridge in a spotless state, polish all the brasswork, keep all the signal flags in good order and finally to steer the ship, especially when entering or leaving ports. In my experience these ratings were the most docile members of the crew and usually ex-Royal Navy men. I don't know what they do to men in the Royal Navy but they turned out some of the most brain-washed people I have ever met.

That is why I was most surprised to find a Quartermaster acting as Ship's Convenor when I joined *Northern Star* a passenger ship which was then employed on fortnightly cruises to the Mediterranean ports. Les Lowe was the only Quartermaster who admitted that he had taken up the role solely because he recognised himself as a naturally indolent person. What made Les unusual to me was his class consciousness and his antipathy towards the officer class. This became the reason for the end of his sea career with the mighty Peninsular & Oriental Shipping Company when they quickly realised that they had an incipient troublemaker on their pay-roll. It seemed obvious to me that he considered himself on par with any of the 'squashed eggs brigade' as he called them, and he certainly lived above his income, with a palatial flat in South Kensington, London. He also dressed expensively and I believe he ran a modern car, which was a good sign of affluence in the 1970s. I never found out where he was educated, but he undoubtedly had the gift of the gab and he certainly used it to good effect in his ship's committee meetings with the obtuse Kiwi skipper of the *Northern Star*. Les was also one of the Southampton delegates on the executive committee of the National Union of Seamen and told me a lot about the antics that went on at Maritime House.

There was also a monetary aspect to the class set-up, because while it was usual to see crew members up before the Skipper to be logged for their acts of indiscipline and disorder, I can't ever remember seeing an officer standing on the 'Carpet' ... in fact I can remember a drunken first mate, who once walloped the captain, on the foredeck of a Geordie tramp, when they had had a difference of opinion over some matter. I discovered later that the mate got off Scot free because it seems that under the Merchant Shipping Acts it is entirely at the discretion of the master as to whether he shall make an entry in the Log Book regarding the misconduct of an officer. It can be seen from this example, that not everyone was equal under the law, at least, not maritime law!

I believe that all these fines and forfeitures were collected at the end of a voyage by the Shipping Master or Marine Superintendent of the Ministry of Transport and forwarded by him to the 'consolidation fund' at the Treasury. These Shipping Masters were supposed to be an impartial referee at the end of a voyage when the crew eventually were discharged and the Articles of Agreement were finally closed. He was supposed to preside over the Pay Off and give even-handed decisions on any dispute between the Master and seamen, but I'm afraid that in my experience, these bureaucrats were mostly biased towards the Master's point of view.

There were three types of report that a seaman could have stamped in his 'Mobile Blacklist' as the Discharge Book was described by some wag; a Very Good, for both conduct and competency, or a Decline to Report, or Endorsement not Required. The last two were looked upon by any possible future employer as a bad Discharge and proof positive of misbehaviour by the applicant for employment in the recent past.

Paddy Neary was the first man to point out to me that if all seamen decided to take an Endorsement not Required discharge, on every occasion, regardless of whatever was being offered by the Shipping Master, it would circumvent the system. Unfortunately, Paddy was the only seaman I know who adopted this method of dislocating the bad discharge arrangement which had been so carefully thought out by our rapacious employers.

I firmly believe that compared to the British shipowner, the Coal Baron and Victorian mill-owners were philanthropists. Their true colours showed through when the South Goodwins Light Vessel broke adrift from her moorings one night in a Force 10 gale, and every crew member was drowned. A relief fund was set up for the benefit of their dependents and the Royal Mail Line (whose ships passed those perilous sands regularly on their way in and out of the port of London) saw fit to contribute, I think it was £250, but it could have been less.

The Discharge Book system, or the voyage report aspect of it, eventually became redundant and also indefensible: I can remember a fireman who received three consecutive double DRs from the same ship, the *New Australia*. The reason for this seeming anomaly was that the owners found it exceedingly difficult to find a crew for this emigrant-cum-troopship, on account of her very bad living quarters for the lower-deck members of the complement. She was also a very warm ship in the Tropics, so much so, that the firemen and greasers had to use pads made of sacking on their hands when descending or climbing the engine room ladders in order to save themselves from being burned. This fireman used to present himself in the Southampton Federation office on the day that he knew the *New Australia* was due to depart from UK and when they couldn't complete the engine room complement, he was signed on at the last minute; and the previous adverse endorsements in his Discharge Book were conveniently ignored ... this happened on two consecutive occasions. As a consequence he finished up with three double DRs.

The worst case I ever heard about was a greaser named Griffiths, who was in a Federal boat which was loading apples in a Tasmanian port. He came back aboard one night full of Aussie plonk, and attacked this inoffensive fellow greaser with a serrated bread knife, causing his victim to go to hospital in a ambulance to get twenty-odd stitches inserted in his skull. The firemen and greasers went after Griffiths to give him a good kicking but he escaped and locked himself in the Captain's cabin, telling the Old Man that he was being persecuted for being anti-Communist and that the rest of the Down-Below crowd were a bunch of Reds. Captain Robin Bell, who of course was known as 'Ding Dong', came down to the firemen's mess and told them that they must allow Griffiths back into the mess and not harm him. The engine-room crowd told him that unless the thug was paid off and sent home, they would be going on strike indefinitely.

On the following day they all walked off the ship and told the wharfies what was happening. Consequently there were no apples loaded that day or the following three days and considering that the sheds which held the cargo were not refrigerated, it looked as though the entire consignment was at risk of going bad. Captain Bell tried to negotiate with the dock labour and a delegation of four wharfies came aboard to hear why he did not think Griffiths should be paid off. He said the man had been taken to court and charged with common assault, for which he had been fined £20, and did not think he should punish the man further. He ended by saying that after all, this was just a Red plot in order to delay the ship. It did not seem to occur to him that out of the dockers' delegation of four, three were Australian Communist Party members and the other was a left-wing Labourite. After a further day of strike action, the message came through from Leadenhall Street to pay the offender off and send him home.

This episode does seem to show that one could get away with murderous assault, provided that one was of the right political complexion. We never learned how Griffiths was dealt with when he reported back to the Establishment Office, but I feel confident that he received a severe slap on the wrist, and was told to be more circumspect in his future dealings with left-wing union activists.

10

The Spoils of War

Anyone who has read this account thus far must be asking themselves why some seamen continued to go to sea under these conditions. The fact is that it became habitual, especially for men who did not like responsibility. Once a seaman had his name on the Articles, problems like where to sleep and eat disappeared, and although the cuisine might not be to one's liking, it did take the wrinkles out of one's belly. Then one could start to criticise the cooks, which was almost *de rigeur* with some characters – usually defectives who would be unable to boil an egg if left to their own devices. Then there was the duty-free cigarettes and tobacco, plus the cheap beer in the 'Pig and Whistle' on the liners. Your wages were strictly controlled by the Master, so there was no chance of one suddenly becoming indigent.

In certain ports where there was no access to shore, the captain, out of the goodness of his heart, would allow local traders to come out to the anchorage with their wares – usually a mixture of electrical goods – and whatever was purchased from them was entered against your account on board. The Master then paid these bumboat men the amounts which had been bought by the crew, remembering to skim a certain percentage off the total for his magnanimity in allowing them to trade on board. I often wonder how may skippers remembered to report these perquisites to the Inland Revenue in the UK!

As one can see, it was a relatively carefree life. Also at the end of the voyage there was a certain wad of mazuma waiting and how big it was depended on how well-behaved or spendthrift one had been during the trip. In addition to what you earned in wages there were also various smuggling enterprises, with which it was possible to supplement one's income.

For instance it was customary for seamen in the Baltic boats to take aboard in the UK large quantities of cheap plonk and sell it at a very healthy profit in Finland, where Finnish alcoholics of both sexes used to scramble aboard, avid to buy all they could get hold of. On the London–Leningrad run, seamen used to go ashore looking like Mr Michelin with four or five woollen pullovers or sweaters and come back aboard shivering in their vests. What they obtained in return for the woollen goods, I'm not sure, but somebody told me that they used to risk a long sojourn in the Gulag for taking religious icons out of Russia!

Business was so lucrative in Franco's Spain that it was very difficult to get a job in Macandrew Line, the regular runners to Portugal and Spain. At one period there were so many Eastern Europeans in these ships, that their crews became known as the Polish Navy. I have heard that large sums of money was paid to certain Pool officials in Dock Street by seamen who badly wanted to get into these ships.

Where the real money was being made was in the four Blue Star boats, known as the 'A' Boats and the Royal Mail Lines' 'Highland Boats'; both of these companies traded regularly to Argentina via the Canary Islands and a carton of American cigarettes purchased for ten shillings in Las Palmas would double its price in Buenos Aires without too much trouble, especially if the local Customs Officers had been squared with a bottle or two of whisky. Of course, as usual, some people got too greedy and instead of cartons of ciggies, it was now cases of them, and this became the norm. Eventually, B.A. Customs raided one of the Blue Star ships and discovered many thousands of Lucky Strikes. Because they could not find the actual smugglers, they fined the ship an exorbitant amount of pesos. The outcome was that Lord Vestey sacked the entire crew, from Commander to Scullion, but the racket still continued.

There must have been scores of rackets going on in the merchant fleet over the years. For instance I know that many seamen in the Manchester Liners brought large amounts of 'King Edward' cigars into the UK for years, and sold them off quite profitably whilst working-by their ships. One bosun I was with in a roll-on-roll-off ferry which was employed on a regular run to Rotterdam's Europoort, with the collusion of a couple of Dutchmen and the lorry drivers, managed to bring huge quantities of Dutch and Belgian cigarette tobacco. It must have been a very widespread and well-organised operation in order to get away with the volumes being smuggled.

The traditional machination for making extra money was the contrivance which entailed the co-operation of the Master, Chief Steward and the ship's Chandler in any given port, and which earned Chief Stewards the nickname of 'Belly robbers'. It worked like this: the steward would submit a long list of comestibles, of which, he told the chandler, he would only need half the quantity to be delivered to the ship! Then in collaboration with the Master he would divide the money saved as a result into three shares, making sure that the Cook got a good drink in order to keep him amenable.

This simple artifice went on for many years and it is said that many Chief Stewards bought rows of houses out of the proceeds of these corrupt practises. Eventually the Shipping Companies woke up to this trickery, and insisted on the transmission of the stores list being sent by radio to their Head Office in UK. Then they would cable the requirements of the ship to their Agents in the relevant port, thus obviating any dishonest behaviour by their faithful servants. Whether this corruption was custom and practise in the Deck and Engine Departments as well, I do not know, but I remember seeing nails, paint, and mooring ropes being sold in the port of Las Palmas on many occasions. As to the Chief Engineer short changing the Company on the amount of oil-bunkers, I am equally ignorant, but I wouldn't be in the least surprised if that proved to be the case.

I was told that any ship that was being taken to the breaker's yard in the Far East was systematically stripped of any brass or copper fitments in the engine room by the engineers, long before the ship arrived at the breakers.

It was during the war though, that the real smuggling went on … millet for bird food was practically unobtainable except on the

Black Market and many thousands of pounds were made by seamen who kept that market supplied, mostly in boats on a regular run to the United States. Other favourite items of contraband were ladies' nylon stockings and Scotch whisky, and of course the old favourites of tobacco and Yankee cigarettes.

11

A Favourite Voyage

The British merchant fleet in its heyday was composed of many different types of ship. There were the Big Ships which were solely employed in the carriage of passengers, owned by such companies as Cunard White Star, Canadian Pacific Railroads, Orient Lines, Peninsular and Oriental Steamship Company, Union Castle Line, Furness Withy Lines and Royal Mail Lines. Most of these firms also owned a fleet of cargo liners in addition to their passenger vessels. New Zealand Shipping Co was combined with the Federal Line to form a large fleet of refrigerated cargo ships employed in the Australasian trade. There were also vast tanker fleets, such as the British Tanker Company, Anglo Saxon Petroleum which later was absorbed into Shell Tankers. There was also a huge number of Esso Tankers, and also Athel Tankers which specialised in carrying loads of molasses in specially lined tanks. Then there was, in addition to the cargo liners, a big fleet of tramp ships which traded world-wide in various cargoes, such as those belonging to Ropners of Cardiff, Chapman Willan of Newcastle, the infamous Baron Boats owned by Hogarths of Greenock, and Stag Boats which hailed from the Tyne, Stephens Sutton, Cairn Line, Lyle Shipping Company from Sunderland. In London the Greek magnates such as Onassis, Hadoulis, Leros and Lehman and others rushed to put their tankers and tramps under the British flag, which was, in fact, a flag of convenience in the 1950s. There was also a vast number of Coasters and Colliers engaged on the short sea trades. To round it up there was also a big fleet of ferry boats owned mainly by British Railways.

Many of the seamen who manned this wide variety of ships stayed in the category of ship in which they felt most at ease. The 'Big Ship man' never felt comfortable unless he had at least 25,000 tons under his feet. 'Tanker-men', despite their hazardous cargoes, became accustomed to the relative cleanliness of tankers when compared to a Tramp ship on a phosphate or coal and iron ore trade. Some seamen gained a degree of security only when they knew that the cargo ship they were in would not be paying off for at least another eighteen months.

Most of the Geordies from South Shields would never have countenanced sailing in anything other than a Collier, whilst some Dover seamen spent their entire sea life criss-crossing the English Channel in the Railway Boats. I myself tried every category at least once, and never visualised being a devotee of any class of ship for any length of time. However, I must say that I have fond memories of at least one cargo ship called *Ramsay* after the poet of that name, and commanded by a grand Old Man called Paddy Kyne who must have been the best skipper I have ever sailed under.

Ramsay was relatively new and belonged to Bolton Steamship Company and she was the first ship I had sailed in with single cabins for all hands. She was also a most stable and comfortable ship, even in very stormy weather. She was on charter to Shaw Savill Line which itself was an adjunct of the mighty Furness Withy Combine.

The charter was for a round voyage to Australia via the Panama Canal outward and homeward via Suez. I was the second cook and baker and the cook was a Scot called Fred Knox.

Fred, who was from Glasgow, was quite an intelligent chap and a very dedicated and competent ship's cook. But he was also something of a Company Man, and never ceased to tell me of his numerous voyages in other ships of the same company, to Monrovia in Liberia on the West Coast of Africa. Unlike other cooks I had sailed with, he did not try to 'Work the Head' on me too much, although I did notice his penchant for putting cornish pasties and steak and kidney pudding on the tea menus for the evening meal. But all in all I was well contented with my berth and actually looked forward to the four-month trip to the main ports on the Australian mainland. *Ramsay* was loaded right down to her marks with general cargo, which we had loaded in Hamburg and London when we cleared the King George V locks at North Woolwich for Panama.

The crew was composed in the main of Middlesbrough men. This was the first time I had sailed with them and they seemed as good as gold on the way out to Aussie, but she was a 'Dry Ship', with no beer and only a weekly tot of rum on Saturday evening for all hands.

It was a far different picture when we arrived in Sydney, after six weeks at sea and the crowd got their first sub and started to sample the Aussie lager. It was like the Gunfight at the OK Corral without the Colt 45s, and there was a lot of blood to be soogeed off the bulkheads the following morning. Fortunately the catering department's cabins were one deck above the crew deck, and although we heard the violent and riotous behaviour into the early hours, we were not physically involved.

What impressed me was the attitude of Captain Kine to this violent interlude. He seemed to acknowledge it as behaviour to be expected from seafarers and his only reaction was to fine those people who the Mate had seen committing damage to the accommodation in the crew quarters. After this first blood-letting, I can't recall any further violent episodes happening during the voyage, apart from the vicious attacks perpetrated by a racehorse which we carried on the after deck along with some pedigree cattle and sheep.

The Irish cattleman was from Roscommon in Eire and although he had no trouble with the cattle, the French stallion called Damtar from M. Boussac's stable refused to have him anywhere near his box. This temperamental thoroughbred managed to bite several people until one of the firemen eventually managed to gain his confidence and was allowed to feed him and clean his horse-box at regular intervals – much to the relief of Paddy the Groom, who compensated the fireman with bottles from the large stock of Irish whiskey he had brought aboard in London when he found out that *Ramsay* was a Dry Ship.

I think I should include a few words about the Chief Steward called Wallace from Aberdeen, who, when he was told by the cook that there wasn't enough kippers to feed both saloon and mess-rooms, instructed Fred to cut the kippers across the back! He often said that he had a Ship's Cook ticket so one Friday afternoon in Melbourne both Fred and I contrived to come back late to cook tea and found that Wallace had set the chip-pan on fire when frying fish.

It was on this voyage that I witnessed an event that was straight out of the sailing ship days. We had returned from Bunbury in Western Australia, light ship, with some timber which we had loaded in that port. We were cruising back and forth across the mouth of Port Philip Bay in foul weather whilst trying to obtain a pilot to take us into Port Melbourne in order to pick up a consignment of wool for Manchester. This patrol had gone on all day until at about four in the afternoon, we made a lee for the Pilot cutter and the old Pilot tied a rope round his waist and, with the other end of the rope secured to our ship, he jumped over into the sea and managed to get hold of our pilot ladder!

This was in mid-winter and it can get very cold in the Port of Melbourne in July. I feel sure the sea must have been icy, plus the fact that these waters are cruising grounds for the Great White Shark. Added to which the ship was rolling violently in the steep waves. We all thought it was a very brave action of the Pilot but he treated it as being part of his job, nonchalantly thanking our deck crowd for their alacrity in pulling him aboard.

It was in this port that the Chief Steward exposed his stupidity by selling all our Canadian flour to some of his friends ashore, and buying some cheap Aussie stuff. He did not seem to be aware that flour from the Antipodes is lacking in gluten and useless for making bread without adding large quantities of flour improver to the dough. Consequently we had small loaves all the way to Aden where he managed to buy some flour improver.

12

Rum, Sodomy and the Lash

I have often thought of this trip and how congenial it was to sail on a Dry Ship, especially when Crew Bars were introduced on British ships a few years later. I first read of this innovation in the Union journal and when I saw that Ronnie Spruhan was praising this development, I immediately thought that this would be a bad thing for British seamen and my worst fears came true. Alcoholism had been prevalent in British ships for many years, but had been confined to Captain, Mates, Chief Engineers, Wireless Operators and Chief Stewards, and was looked upon as an occupational disease. With the advent of Crew Bars, which in most cases were open all day and night, the complaint became endemic – with the consequent increase in suicides, violence, insubordination, accidents, and a general lowering of the quality of life on board.

I once gained access to a Report Book of disciplinary hearings held over a period of months in the Tilbury Establishment Office, and after reading it all through, I discovered that in 90 per cent of the cases of crime and various malfeasances, alcohol had been the root cause of the trouble. I honestly believe that this joint decision by the shipowners and their union was verging on the criminal. It was akin to putting pyromaniacs in charge of a munitions factory. The introduction of Crew Bars also gave unscrupulous characters a chance to exploit the financial aspects of running a bar, thereby increasing their earnings by considerable amounts of tax-free loot. I kept asking myself what was the reason for this show of liberality on the part of the shipowners?

This radical change in the shipowners' attitude towards drinking aboard ship caused me much cogitation. From a previously strict rationing system of two cans of beer per day for crew members, there was now suddenly a license to indulge oneself day or night in consuming unlimited amounts of not only strong beer, but spirits as well. It was incomprehensible to me for a long time, before I realised that the embryonic, on-board trade union activities, which had been fought over for years and bitterly opposed by the employers, had now become virtually defunct.

The so-called Shipboard Representation Scheme had been watered down from its inception because the position of Convenor was at the bestowal of the local Union officials and not by election of the members. Of course the officials made sure that the position was placed in safe hands. The Convenor was then supposed to call an election meeting for the installation of the departmental delegates, but usually the Convenor prevailed on a couple of his friends to take the jobs, or simply did not even bother to call any meetings, which made his life that much more congenial.

I must be honest and admit that the scheme had never been embraced with the greatest of enthusiasm by the majority of seamen, and in no way encouraged by the Master and so-called officers aboard the various ships in which it was introduced. This scheme became much less attractive when it became known that some diligent Convenors had been sacked and victimised because of their efforts aboard some of the big ships. I found it hard to realise that the shipowners would be prepared to accept all the ensuing trouble and general mayhem which followed the introduction of Crew Bars in return for the liquidation of the Shipboard Representation Scheme; but that in fact was what did actually happen.

It would be interesting to discover how many deaths and suicides could be attributed to the licentiousness and debauchery which became the norm as a result of this relaxation of shipboard discipline – but one case does stick in my memory. A Galley Boy was lost overboard from one of Tate and Lyle's 'sugar boats' just as she was leaving Santos, Brasil. It seemed that the Crew Bar had run out of beer, due to a very heavy session on sailing day as a celebration of their departure for London River. The Second Cook and Baker, a real lush, had taken it upon himself to 'borrow' some beer from the Engineers Bar situated on the deck above the Crew

Bar, and he told the Galley Boy to keep a look-out for any engineers while he did the borrowing. It appeared that the lad, who had had a few drinks, climbed on the taff-rail and holding on to the coaming, gained a direct view into the Engineers' accommodation. Unfortunately he slipped off the rail and plunged into the wake of the vessel, and although the propellors were only turning at half speed at that time, he must have become entrapped in their blades. Although the boat was launched, no one found a trace of the unfortunate lad. The Chief Superintendent of the Tilbury Mercantile Marine Office went aboard with the boy's parents when the ship came to anchor in the Thames to conduct an enquiry into the death and returned a verdict of accidental death. However, he must have suspected something when he saw the amounts of cash that the lad had been drawing at sea (also an innovation to maritime life) because the money could only have been spent mostly in the Crew Bar at sea.

I know this account to be correct because I met the Second Cook and Baker who was involved in the accident when he paid off and started to drown his guilty conscience in a pub known as 'Bum Daddy' facing the Queen Victoria Seamen's Rest on the East India Dock Road, in 1974.

There was also the case of two stewards in one of the Royal Mail A Boats. I forget their names, but they could have been called William Fitzpatrick and Patrick Fitzwilliam. It would seem that one of these love-birds became insanely jealous when he found out that his chum was having dalliances with another homo, and having got himself full of 'Widows Ruin' in the Crew Bar, he turned on his ex-paramour with an ice-pick, in their cabin one night. The result was that his lover rapidly became deceased, and their ex-love nest resembled an abattoir.

13

The Decline of the Red Duster

I make no apologies at this juncture for reproducing a short excerpt from the monthly journal of the National Union of Seamen, entitled *Britain's Money-making MN* from February 1966.

In 1964 the 2,500 deep-sea ships of Britain's Merchant Navy earned more than £900 million. Some 55 per cent of our exports and 48 per cent of our imports were shipped under the 'Red Duster'. So it is easy to see why shipping is indispensable to Britain's economy (writes Montague Lacey, Daily Express) *in an article illustrated by impressive facts and figures. Our Merchant Navy, with its 20,500,000 tons of shipping, mainly modern, is, he claims, the largest active merchant fleet in the world, and a gigantic asset which has a replacement value of about £3,600 million at present-day prices. But here comes a warning note: 'It is alarming,' says the writer 'that our sea trade is slipping away. The erosion has become noticeable in the last decade.'*

Two reasons for this are advanced. One is the increasing competition from foreign shipping, much of it subsidised. The other is uncertain and late deliveries from British exporters. In the same feature, Alan Grainge shows the distribution of the export trade in terms of sterling, between the 15 principal ports. London tops the bill, with about £1,500 million a year. Liverpool's total is £930 million. Next comes Hull (£230 million), Glasgow (£160 million)

66

and Manchester (£130 million). The total value of the country's exports comes to about £4,000 million a year.

After reading such authoritative data, surely the reader could be forgiven for asking why such an important and wealth producing industry had not been nationalised when the Labour Government came into office in 1945 on the back of a landslide election victory, instead of taking into public ownership such bankrupt businesses as the railway system and the obsolete coal mines! Such questions always bring to mind the oft-repeated saying of George Holloway, a very percipient character from Dagenham, who when the topic of the Labour Party entered the conversation, was apt to say 'The only thing that the Labour Party has done consistently since its inception, is to stab the British working class in the back, and they are still doing it.'

They certainly never addressed the problems of British shipping when they were in office, for instance the encroachment of the Free Flag fleets, the taking over of the British coastal trades by foreign flag vessels and the steady run-down of the ferry boats which came under the management of British Railways. One could possibly argue that the Conservative governments of those years when they were in power, were equally remiss in their stewardship of the British merchant fleet – but surely that was to be expected of these advocates of the free market forces, with their creed of non-interference in the affairs of capitalism. In retrospect one can only conclude that all the political parties were culpable in the gradual liquidation of the world's biggest merchant fleet. There is no doubt in my mind that the creation of massive fleets under the flags of Liberia, Panama, Honduras and Costa Rica is no more or less than a licence for shipowners to drown seamen with *carte blanche*, much as they did when they sent the 'Coffin Ships' to sea, in the days before Samuel Plimsoll became active in the welfare of seamen. I had occasion to visit some of those Free Flag ships in the 1970s, in company with John Nelson, the Manchester branch secretary, who was also one of the International Transport Federation's British representatives, and I was appalled by some of the foul conditions these Third World seamen were forced to live under in these rustbuckets.

One example of this flagrant maritime decrepitude was an ex-

P&O Coast Lines vessel, which had been 'Flagged Out' and was now employed under the Panamanian flag, running phosphate from North Africa to Eccles on the Manchester Ship Canal. Nelson took me into one of the AB's cabins to show me a West African seaman huddled shivering under one cotton blanket and lying on two wooden planks with no springs or mattress to lie on. It was January and quite chilly, but the steam radiator was disconnected from the steam line and just leaning against the bulkhead. Whilst Nelson was negotiating with the English skipper, I took the opportunity to have a close look at the ship's life-boats and discovered that neither of them could be lowered overside, due to the fact that the rope falls were painted so thickly that it would have been impossible for them to pass through the blocks. I tried to get Nelson to get the ship held up, pending repairs, but he said that the Ministry of Transport would not act in this matter.

Having read this dissertation so far, the reader could be forgiven for suspecting the author of extreme prejudice towards the NUS, which I would accept, but I also realise that it was in the beginning a worthy opponent of the employers, until it became corrupted by the shipowners, I think during the First World War, when they saw that Havelock Wilson (Founder President of NUS) under certain circumstances would act against the best interests of his members. The classic example was his refusal to oppose the stopping of allotment notes when the ship became a casualty in the war at sea, a custom which continued during the Second World War twenty years later.

I feel quite sure that at some time in the 1920s, Wilson and his cohorts decided that if they could not beat the British shipowners, it was as well to join them, and that unholy alliance continued to be advantageous to both parties over the next fifty years. Until, that is, the owners realised that it was more profitable to put their ill-gotten gains into less risky businesses, such as insurance companies and construction firms. In any case by the 1970s the growth of the Free Flag fleets was so phenomenal that they found that they couldn't compete with them in the bulk and tanker markets. Some of the British owners built huge container vessels, ships which could carry in metal boxes the cargo equivalent to that which used to be carried by six conventional ships – with the consequent reduction in the number of seamen needed to man this fleet. How the shipowners managed to dispense with the services of these surplus seamen without paying out substantial amounts of redundancy money to them, is yet another disgraceful episode in the history of the British shipping industry.

For the purpose of deleting the workforce, the owners enlisted the services of the 'men in the white coats', i.e. the Pool doctors. These gentlemen of the Hippocratic Oath had no compunction in declaring seamen unfit for further sea service, which obviated the need for the employer to pay any kind of severance payment. It is my firm and sincere belief that thousands of employees were dealt with in this dastardly manner over a few years.

I myself was declared unfit because of hypertension in 1976, and went on to do another ten years at sea in New Zealand merchant ships!

Once again the NUS proved invaluable in this infamous behaviour. I have never heard of one case where the Union successfully challenged one of these illegal expulsions and it was noticeable how the militants were the first to go. But anyone was grist to the mill, once the rationalisation of the British Merchant fleet got under way. I don't know how the officer class fared in this bloodbath: and I do not really care.

14

The Wanderer Returns

In 1958 after hanging on in the Auckland Sailors Home for some weeks, I had succeeded in gaining membership in the New Zealand Seamen's Union and made a couple of trips as Motorman to South Australia in a grain ship until she laid up in Auckland. Her name was *Wairoa* and she was a good ship. Then I got a job in a collier called *Kaitawa,* which was on a regular trade carrying coal from Westport in the South Island to the power station in Auckland. She was also a good berth, but after a couple of voyages, she also laid up for the Christmas and New Year holidays.

It was then that I heard about a ship called *Riseley,* a British tramp, owned by Stephens Sutton of Newcastle. She was lying in New Plymouth and I flew down from Auckland to join her as second steward. This was the worst mistake that I have ever made because I finished up six months later being left behind in the port of Colon in Panama, losing all my gear and wages. I still have nightmares about this Geordie tramp nearly forty years later, and find that the time I spent in her is too painful to write about.

I came back to UK in the *Athelduchess,* a molasses carrier returning to Birkenhead from a trip to Hawaii. Before I left Auckland I had 'hung up my union book' in the proper manner so that I could continue sailing in New Zealand ships in the future if I so chose to.

So in 1974 I took passage in a Russian passenger ship to Auckland via South Africa and Australia and landed in New

Zealand just before Christmas with a few hundred pounds in my pockets, and raring to get back into the sea game once again. Unfortunately for me, there had been a drastic change in the attitude of New Zealanders towards the British since Britain had joined the European Common Market, which caused much damage to the NZ economy, and forced them to look for alternative markets for their fruit and frozen meat exports. So when I applied to pick up my union book, I received a chilly reception from the New Zealander who was then secretary of the Auckland branch. Consequently I was hanging around unemployed until March 1976, except for a few nightwatchmen's jobs on ships that the New Zealand watchmen didn't care to take. Eventually I got tired of waiting and took a job as assistant/pantryman in the *Ocean Monarch*, a Shaw Savill liner which was en-route to the UK via Panama, prior to being broken up in Taiwan. This again turned out to be another lousy experience.

When I arrived home I found that my registration on the Manchester Pool had been revoked, and I spent nine months on the dole, before John Nelson, the Manchester branch secretary of the NUS, managed to fix me up with a cook steward's job in the sludge boats belonging to the North West Water Authority. These four ships were based at Barton on the Manchester Ship Canal, and carried treated sludge from the Waterworks at Urmston down the Ship Canal to be dumped in the outer reaches of the River Mersey in Liverpool Bay. I was employed as relief cook steward but when the four regular men were working in their ships, I was then deployed as assistant steward to clean the officers' cabins and wait on them at table.

This arrangement did not go down with me at all well — I think it contributed to the 'Bolshie' attitude which I developed over the next two years, and which served to separate me from the rest of the labour force. These were without doubt the most servile bunch of seamen I ever had the misfortune to work with. Even when it became clear to all hands that the controller, an arrogant bully, was deliberately favouring one crew out of the four employed, namely the ship which had the Union Convenor aboard, nobody was prepared to do anything about the unfair situation. This included the Manchester Branch Secretary, Brother Nelson, who at that time was too involved in trying to get justice for Free Flag crews, who were not even members of his organisation.

During these two years I was involved in litigation with Shaw Savill Line, who had refused to repatriate me to New Zealand after the *Ocean Monarch* voyage, regardless of the fact that I had a permanent residence visa for New Zealand in my passport. I won the case after two years, but all that I received, after the lawyer had taken his bite of the cherry, was a couple of hundred pounds – just enough to buy me a one-way ticket to Auckland. By this time I had managed to procure another New Zealand visa, and decided to make another attempt to get back on the NZ coast ... so it was with some trepidation that I climbed into a Quantas Jumbo 747 and took off once again for the Antipodes. This time when I applied to pick up my NZ union book it was a Maori chap who was in the post of Auckland secretary and more sympathetic to my plight. After keeping me hanging round for a few weeks in the Auckland Sailors Home, whilst he was checking my bona fides, he eventually installed me in *Kaitawa* and away we went across the Tasman to Port Pirie in the Spencer Gulf for a load of copper ingots. I stayed in this ship for a couple of trips until she laid up prior to being sold.

My next ship was a ten thousand ton natural gas tanker named *Kotuku* which I believe was owned by a Greek shipowner and managed on a long-term charter by the Union Steamship Company of New Zealand. We used to pick up the cargo of condensate gas, which is a natural petroleum and very volatile with an extremely low flashpoint, from the port of New Plymouth in the province of Taranaki, where the gas was piped ashore from the off-shore gas rig for the Maui gas field. I must admit that I felt a tad uncomfortable with this dangerous trade, but she was such a good job that I stayed in her for a long time, until I had so much money in the bank that I felt more secure than I had for years.

By this stage I was out of the Sailors Home and living in a spacious two-bedroomed flat in Onehunga, which is on the Eastern side of the isthmus from Auckland. I had procured a mortgage from a lawyer in that town and had paid it off within a year and a half, so I had a real place of security when the NZ economy took a dive a couple of years after I arrived.

When I eventually left the gas tanker, I managed to get a job on one of two Paper Boats. These ships were built specially for the carriage of large rolls of newsprint from the port of Mount Maunganui near Tauranga to various ports on the Australian mainland, plus two ports in Tasmania. It was in one of these ships that I encountered Bluey Davis, a first generation New Zealander, and virulently anti-British, as well as being a fanatical Labour party supporter. He gave a whole new meaning to the phrase 'jaundiced bigotry'. In direct contrast, and in the same ship, was an assistant steward called Barney Kennedy who was still very much a Scouse despite residing in New Zealand for many years.

He had started out on deck in British ships as a lad and jumped ship in Wellington in order to begin work in New Zealand vessels in the deck department, but failing eyesight had forced him to change over to being a steward.

He had the largest repertoire or jokes and one-liners of anyone I have known, and would entertain one with these at great length. It was he who told me that most Liverpool dockers were given nicknames by their workmates, but only two names stuck in my memory. One was the young docker who worked in the same gang as his father and who got into the habit, at midday, of shouting down the hatchway, in whichever ship he and his father happened to be working, 'Tell me Da, I'm shooting up to Ma's for dinner'. He was promptly christened the 'Spaceman'. Another stevedore who, when called upon to trim the ship's derricks in order to facilitate cargo handling, would begin shouting to other dockers in his gang; 'Release that guy' or 'Let that guy go', became known thereafter as 'The lenient judge'.

On one occasion in a packed messroom, Barney tried to convince me that a certain docker who had been taking his mid-morning tea break in one of the dockside canteens, had just sat down with his mug of tea and a custard tart, when a large flake of rust fell from a girder above and hit him on the head, some of which finished up in his custard. Being a litigious type, he took the problem to a lawyer in Liverpool called Livermore, who was well known in the port as the 'Docker's QC' and who would take on any kind of compensation case for dock-workers.

At the end of the interview with the docker client, Livermore is supposed to have said that he was somewhat perplexed as to what title he should put on this brief. After a moment's thought the docker supposedly replied 'What about calling it, "The Case of the Rusty Custard?"' Barney kept a perfectly straight face throughout the telling of this preposterous tale, despite the mess-room being convulsed with laughter.

It was a good thing that there were people like Barney at sea, if only to alleviate the tensions raised by the Bluey Davis's of this world. In fact there was a continual underlying tension; due to the fact that the deck department formed the majority of the membership and were thus able to ensure that the Executive Council of the union was composed mainly of able-seamen, in addition to which most of the shipboard delegates were also either able-seamen or bosuns. This was very noticeable when attending the union stop-work meetings which were held monthly in the major ports throughout New Zealand. The engine-room ratings would probably be most vociferous in the meetings, but when it came to the vote it was usually the deck department point of view which gained the decision. I often wonder what happened after I retired when the Seamen's Union amalgamated with the Cooks and Stewards Union.

The aspect of NZ seagoing which was most attractive to me, i.e. one month on and one month off, was because it meant that one received one year's salary for six months work! It really was a good set up because the overtime payments were built into the fortnightly wage, and for the first time in my seagoing career, I felt that I was at last being paid what I was worth. With the first-class accommodation and excellent food we received, I considered myself to be very fortunate to be in such congenial circumstances. My only regret is that I did not take advantage of the time off and improve my academic education at Auckland University. I still can't figure out why I let this great opportunity pass me by, because by this time I had solved my drink problem, given up tobacco and had no inclination to take up the national pastime of betting on stupid race horses.

I found it an idyllic set up with the sub-tropical climate and the only reservation I had was about the attitudes of the indigenous population who seemed to have contempt for people with intelligence, or who even used words of more than three syllables. If one didn't drink or gamble and have an expert knowledge of the game of rugby one was considered way outside the pale.

One such person was a Scotsman called John Devitt, who seemed to have divorced himself from 95 per cent of his fellow workers, and who despite being a strict teetotaler was nevertheless a compulsive gambler on the horses. After a few years he seemed to recognise me as a kindred spirit and I well remember the oft-repeated stories of his exploits during the Second World War in which he served in the Highland Light Infantry and Lovats Scouts. He used to relate with relish the actions he was engaged in during the post D-Day landings, when the Allied armies were fighting to burst out of the Normandy bridgehead. He was the only ex-soldier I have ever met who really seemed to enjoy being involved in armed conflict.

After eight years I was offered the 'golden handshake' and accepted with alacrity when I realised how long I had been involved in seafaring without even getting my socks wet.

The incident which finally made me decide to return to England permanently however, was the "Mount Erebus' disaster, in which one of Air New Zealand's DC10s on an excursion flight to Antarctica ploughed into the above named mountain with a consequent loss of all the crew and passengers!

This led to the setting up by the prime minister, Sir Robert Muldoon, of a government commission of enquiry and the installation as commissioner of a New Zealand Judge named Justice Mahon, an excellent jurist of integrity and a man who pursued the cause of the disaster with the utmost conscientiousness – even to the extent of going to the USA and Britain to garner evidence in order to come to a correct conclusion in regard to this horrendous accident. As I remember it now, it seemed that the Air New Zealand top management was confidently asserting that the crash was solely and completely due to pilot error and they were blameless. But it turned out during the enquiry that a member of the management had changed the flight co-ordinates on the airline's computer, without bothering to advise the pilots of this fact. As a consequence the pilot was under the impression that he was flying his aircraft safely down MacMurdo Sound when actually the plane was on a collision course for the volcano called Mount Erebus!

When Justice Mahon finally published his report, which found the airline completely culpable of the calamity, a very strange event took place when the media, the government and large sections of the population took umbrage at his decision to the extent that the eminent judge was forced to take the government to the New Zealand High Court and sue them for defamation of his character! To me these incredible happenings were completely mind-boggling. Here was a man of the utmost probity, who had made a very scrupulous enquiry into this catastrophe over a period of some months, and finally brought in a logical verdict, only to be castigated by the majority of the New Zealand populace because they thought that his findings cast aspersions on the state airline!

I had seen some examples of chauvinism in my travels but nothing to equal this institutional madness. In fact I had formed the strong belief based on what I had observed on my worldly peregrinations that I was in fact living on a lunatic planet and what I have witnessed since has only strengthened my belief that this is an incontrovertible fact of life. One has only to cast an objective eye over the history of the past hundred years in order to become convinced of this truth.

To quote a few examples of the genocidal acts which have taken place in the 19th and 20th centuries ... the Irish Potato Famine which killed thousands by hunger, and was completely unnecessary ... the decimation of the North American Indians by the US Army ... the outright slaughter of indigenous peoples in numerous countries, such as Australia, Argentina, Mexico and the Atzecs and Mayan cultures ... Stalin and Mao Tse Tung along with Pol Pot have millions of deaths on their heads ... the six million Jews who were consumed in the German Nazi Holocaust ... the twenty million Soviet citizens killed in the Second World War ... the genocide in Armenia.

There is almost no place on earth where man has not shown his lust for mayhem and bloodletting on a global scale. He has also proved himself to be the most pollutive species this planet has ever spawned and worse still, has shown that he is fully capable of completely destroying the cosmos itself, and which I firmly believe he is in the process of doing.

I have long held the belief that the world is a gyrating lunatic asylum, but recently I have amended this notion somewhat to the credence that the situation is even worse, inasmuch that it seems that the worst afflicted lunatics seem to be in complete control of the institution in these times.

I realise that this assertion has probably been made many times over the centuries, but this does not alter the incontestable fact of global warming and the increasing pollution of the small seas and the great oceans, which places the planet in a more perilous state than has been the case over many aeons of time.

GLOSSARY

Old Man	=	captain/shipmaster
Harry Tate	=	first mate
Doocer	=	second engineer or second steward
Belly robber	=	chief steward
Doc	=	ship's cook
Hunk or cowboy	=	assistant steward
Pisspot jerker	=	bedroom steward
Sparks	=	wireless operator
Bosun	=	sheriff
Chippie	=	carpenter
Topside men	=	barmen, lounge and smokeroom stewards
Ladies fever	=	veneral disease
Catching the boat up	=	contracting VD
The black pan	=	special fry-up meal for the 4 pm to 8 pm watches. Served at 8–10 pm
Seven bells breakfast and dinner	=	Served at 7.20 am for 8 am to noon watch and at 11.25 am for noon to 4 pm watch
Tabbies	=	stewardesses
A no mark	=	person beneath contempt
Person with fingers all the same length	=	thief
Made up	=	well pleased
Woolly backs	=	Persons from outside Liverpool

Got the hammer	=	got torpedoed
On the hook	=	ships at anchor
Got legless	=	became intoxicated
Having a bevy	=	imbibing alcohol
Baling out or skinning out	=	act of desertion
Pay day	=	end of voyage pay-off
A Nipper	=	one who borrows small amounts at regular intervals, with no intention of repaying them
A note cracker	=	one who cashes seamen's advance notes at 30 per cent discount
Down by the head	=	heavy laden
Blue flue	=	Blue Funnel Line
Cunard feet	=	splayed and flat feet
Conny honey	=	tinned condensed milk
Pea wack	=	split pea soup
Jack the Rippers	=	kippers
Sam boat	=	Wartime-built "Liberty Ship' built in United States
Abadan blues	=	Mental aberration suffered by tanker men
Skin boats	=	Elder & Fyffes banana ships
Sandy MacNabs	=	crab lice
Mobile dandruff	=	as above
Bat and biff	=	syphilis
Burgoo	=	porridge oats
Donkey's breakfast	=	straw-filled mattress purchased by old-time sailors and firemen
Panhandler	=	mendicant or bum
Putting the bite on someone	=	begging
Lowering the boom	=	as above
Stack of bricks	=	Empire Memorial Seamen's Hostel, Commercial Road, London, E14
Stornaway castle	=	Flying Angel Seamen's Hostel, Victoria Dock Road, London, E16

Queen Vic	=	Seamen's Rest, East India Dock Road, London, E14
Red Ensign Club	=	Sailors' Home, Dock Street, London E1
Pound and pint	=	Basis of seamen's scale of rations
Cement pocket	=	One who is slow to pay his round in a bar
Mazuma	=	ready cash
Loot	=	as above
A snide	=	sneak, telltale, bosses' man
Hallelujah bum	=	seamen who frequent religious services in sailors' homes for gain
A rosie	=	a bucket or receptacle for disposal of food left-overs
Gash bucket	=	as above
Human rosie	=	gluttonous person
Tab-nabs	=	cakes and confectionery
Board of Trade duff	=	steamed fruit pudding
Soogee moogee	=	liquid made up for washing paint-work
Holystones	=	sandstones attached to long handles for whitening deck planking
Red lead	=	tomato soup
Jaspers	=	cockroaches or steam flies
Joe shell	=	the Shell Tanker Group
Spud barber	=	galley boy
Skin and eye specialist	=	as above
Glory-hole steward	=	person who cleans the catering department accommodation
Pearl divers	=	plate house gang on liners
Quack	=	ship's doctor
Strap up	=	washing up plates and utensils
Skipper's tiger	=	captain's steward
Channel money	=	Cash paid out to crew just prior to arrival in UK to pay any custom duty

Burn down	=	ship's firemen's name for a double decline to report
The Liverpool splash	=	a method of spraying coal on to boiler fires, in order to raise steam pressure faster
Taking the deep six	=	description of burial at sea
Gone for a burton	=	deceased, defunct
Working alleyway	=	main access on large liners between forward and aft
Living Caso	=	man and woman living together outside marriage
Under Australian articles	=	as above
Slipped him a Mickey Finn	=	Added drug to person's drink
A mush	=	A denizen of Southampton
The rags A cathouse A knocking shop	=	names for brothels
Mama San	=	Madam of Japanese brothel
Sky pilot	=	clergyman
Yoxies	=	seamen from south end of Liverpool, who speak with a peculiar accent
A big nine-cylinder job	=	description of an overweight woman

APPENDIX I

The Story of Havelock Wilson, 1859–1929

Havelock Wilson, founder-president of the NUS was one of the most forceful and creative personalities in the British trade union movement. The story of his struggles, defeats, and ultimate enduring success is told in the following abridged article by Frank Taylor, who was a young seafarer who took a course in political science and economics at Ruskin College, Oxford, and there gained a scholarship which took him for twelve months to Australia. He is now serving as a Dock Delegate of the Union in the Victoria and Albert Docks branch, London.

Joseph Havelock Wilson was born in Sunderland in 1859, the son of a master draper. He was still a child when his father died, and at an early age he was on the streets selling newspapers to help the family income. Like other boys in seaports, he used to spend many hours hanging around the docks, no doubt dreaming and hoping for the time when he would be old enough to sail away. He and a mate did make one early venture as ship's crew, but this was brought to a sudden close when they were reported missing by their parents. When eventually he did go to sea and suffered all the usual happenings which befell seamen in those days – being out of work for long periods, having to accept different rates of pay in ships from different ports, being stranded ashore in overseas ports if he were unlucky enough to fall sick on the voyage, sailing under primitive conditions with shipmasters of various types, yet always going back to sea after a few days or weeks ashore.

In those days there were no uniform rates of pay. There was no overtime; hours were worked as required. Crimping was wide-spread, especially on the American coast, and food scales, accommodation and the like would depend on the type of Company one sailed in, and the Master one sailed under. There was no redress for a seaman against his misfortune, real or imaginary.

This was Havelock Wilson's initiation, and apprenticeship, which it will be as well to remember when weighing up the methods he used himself in later life. Wilson tells in his autobiography how he joined the Australian Seamen's Union, and when he came home he went along and joined the local Seamen's Union in Sunderland. This was purely a local organisation with not much in the way of finance, membership, or influence.

Prior to the late 1880s the industrial organisation of seamen was practically non-existent, with the exception of these few minor and (relatively) inefficiently organised 'Unions' in London, Hull, and Sunderland. Attempts by the TUC to form a seamen's union on Clydeside earlier in the century failed. So the Sunderland Union was rather weak, but Wilson with youth and vigour on his side did much to bolster up the branch. Previously the only people to attend the Union meetings had been retired 'shellbacks' and loafers; as a result of Wilson's activity, interest among the younger men greatly increased. Yet the main difficulty from both the Union's and Wilson's point of view was that from the time he sailed till the time he came home again the Union underwent a period of slump, and then had a periodic revival. This situation continued for some time, until at last the issue was forced by an outside influence – his wife, who had been trying to get him to come ashore because the family had decided to open a small cafe or coffee shop, and Wilson was to be included in the new arrangements.

So in 1886, Wilson 'swallowed the anchor', and came ashore. It certainly cannot be said that his first efforts as organiser were crowned with success. After many enquiries and much hard work, he had handbills printed and made it known within the Sunderland area that the inaugural meeting of a National Union was to take place.

The meeting was a complete flop; the total attendance was exactly two, Wilson and one other. This may have daunted a lesser man, but only served to spur Wilson on. He duly enrolled the other man and himself as the first two members of the union, to be known by the grand title of 'The National Amalgamated Sailors' and Firemen's Union of Great Britain and Ireland'.

The following week another meeting was arranged, and this time there was a better attendance. The National Union for Seamen had arrived. By the end of the year (1888), it affiliated to the TUC with 500 members.

During 1888, Wilson was extremely busy covering the many ports of the country, starting up branches of his National Union, and in doing so, laid the foundations for its failure.

In his autobiography he ruefully concedes that he tried to do too much. The basic trouble was that he had taken on more than he could efficiently manage and this was to bring about the downfall of his cherished Union.

By this time he had attracted the attention of Samuel Plimsoll, and became involved in the political activities of unionism. After a turbulent strike in Cardiff (Wilson received six weeks in jail for his efforts there) he was nominated for a seat in the House of Commons. This was at Deptford, where he was beaten. He was then nominated for Bristol, but withdrew, to stand at Middlesbrough and was duly returned. He sat as MP for Middlesbrough from 1892 to 1900, and again from 1906 to 1910. From 1918 to 1922 he was member for South Shields.

That he did useful work for seamen in Parliament cannot be denied. He sat on numerous Royal Commissions, including those on the Manning of British Merchant Vessels, the Tonnage of Merchant Vessels, the extension of Workmen's Compensation Acts to seamen and also the Commission on Boy Seamen.

Wilson was extremely pleased with the work of the 1905 Commission, which extended the Workmen's Compensation Act to seamen, yet oddly enough later on in life he had no time at all for the political side of unionism. By this time he had stimulated the employers to form their own organisation.

In 1890 the Shipping Federation Limited had been registered as a company, but it is freely admitted that it was created to combat the growing threat of organised seamen. One of Wilson's beliefs was that once the shipowners did organise themselves, agreement between the two sides would be reached more easily than if the Union had to deal with individual ship owners.

Among his ideas was the suggestion that shipowners should fix a standard price for freight, which would enable them to pay standard wage rates in all ships. Meanwhile, union activity went on.

Branches of the union were opened on the continent as early as 1889, with one in Germany, followed by others in Antwerp, Rotterdam, and then one in Denmark. These branches were intended primarily to give help to seamen's organisations in those countries. Wilson worked on the idea that once these other seamen were organised, their ways would become standardised, and it would lessen the possibilities of cheap labour being available.

With all these ventures going on, it was not surprising that administrative tasks did not get as much of Wilson's time as was needed, and the result was its gradual disintegration.

By 1894 – in Wilson's own words – the union was on its last legs, and writs were being showered on it. Various people and organisations had managed to get hold of credit notes on the union, but Wilson forestalled them, and went into voluntary liquidation.

As soon as its affairs were wound up, Wilson started up the next round of the struggle, and formed the National Sailors' and Firemen's Union. He had now seven years of practical experience behind him – an appropriate length of time for an apprenticeship.

The next stage of Wilson's efforts can be divided into two main periods, firstly while he was still active, and secondly the period his life when he became increasingly dependent on others to do his field work. From 1894 to approximately 1910, he was still able to get about, and he continued his work in Parliament. One achievement of this time was the passing of the 1906 Merchant Shipping Act of that year.

Meanwhile, on the industrial side he was still trying to get the Shipping Federation to recognise the Union. This the Federation steadfastly refused to do, and from their point of view this was quite understandable.

There was at this time various 'Unions' in existence, the main one for the lower deck being Wilson's Union, and one known as Cotter's Union (after its leader Joseph Cotter). The official name of this union was The National Union of Ship's Stewards, Cooks, Butchers and Bakers and it had a membership of about one third the total of the Sailors' and Firemen's Union. As one might expect, it was drawn mainly from the ports of Southampton, Liverpool and London. Yet, although rivalry was very certainly keen between each union, the main threat was always kept for the employers.

It is possible here to see why Wilson rarely mentioned what he actually sailed as when he was at sea. He does say on one occasion that he sailed as a second mate in a Baltic trader, but in the main he sailed as Able Seaman Cook (Certified Ship's Cooks were not carried until after the passing of the 1906 MS Act).

The new Union progressed very well, and Wilson's efforts to establish support abroad were kept up. In 1909 an International Conference of Seafarers was held, and many demands were put forward, among them a demand for a National Negotiating and Wages Board to consider a manning scale for ships, hours of work, and accommodation problems. These demands were refused in all the seven countries where they were put forward, and consequently an international seamen's strike was called for June 1911.

Rheumatoid arthritis was now seriously impeding Wilson's movements, and it was shortly to make him a complete invalid. He therefore engaged Edward Tupper, who led the Strike, particularly in the Cardiff area. But always behind Tupper was the figure of Wilson, the real director. In fact Tupper had no previous knowledge of the sea: he was an ex-army man.

The Strike of 1911 was a qualified success. On June 26th, just before it started, the Shipping Federation said to the Union: 'We will not recognise the Union as they are not representative of all seamen.' Yet by July 21st, although the Union's demands had not all been successful, they had been granted recognition. But much remained to be done. Wilson's main obstacle was that there was no negotiating machinery to enable owners and men to discuss their differences. Strangely enough the next, and possibly to Wilson, the final step came when seamen were in a very strong bargaining position during the First World War. Some claims that were advanced by the Union were met, but if any demands were refused, Wilson would do nothing but put them forward again. His militancy seemed to evaporate at this time, and the Strike as a weapon was placed into cold storage for the duration.

With an almost fanatical patriotism he was more concerned to collect crews for the ships than to cash in on their shortage. Among other things that caused much bitterness, was the stopping of allotments the moment a ship was posted as missing with the families being left destitute. This was a very sore point at the start of the war with seamen, but Wilson would never consider using the ultimate weapon to force the issue.

In the meantime, shipping freights had risen by as much as 400 per cent. But Wilson would not act on this, except by way of negotiation.

By 1917, the shortage of seamen to man ships had become so acute that it led to the settlement of the final bone of contention between the shipowners and the men. In August of that year a meeting was held under the auspices of the Ministry of Shipping. All sat down together, including owners and Unions, to consider what could be done to improve the supply of merchant seamen. By November of the same year a draft had been completed, and a constitution agreed for a Board to be set up to consider these problems. The Unions managed to have included within its terms of reference a claim for action at national level on wages and standard rates of pay. This was a breakthrough. The Board was set up, only for the duration of the war and the transition period afterwards, but it meant that the deadlock was broken.

The Board worked quite well from its inception, and when the war had been over for a year it was agreed by both sides that it should be continued as a Joint Industrial Council. In 1920 there was a new constitution, and it became the National Maritime Board. On it were included representatives of the Liverpool shipowners and the Railway Companies. The only major change was that the referring of disputes to the Shipping Controller was abandoned.

There were to be three levels of the new board – at local port level there were Port Consultants, who could define rules and agreements, but not alter them. If they could not give a ruling they *would then pass the dispute on to the top level, the National Maritime Board, which again was divided into sub-sections of the various departments concerned, e.g. Deck, Engine, Catering and Navigating etc.*

Since the inception of the Board there has never been an official Strike in the industry, which seems to support Wilson's belief that once men and owners got together over a problem, it could be satisfactorily settled between them.

The next serious threat to the strength of the Unions came from within. In 1921 during the slump that occurred after the First World War, all the Seamen's Unions agreed to take a cut in pay, but at the last minute Cotter's Union refused, and went on strike. But the result was inevitable, and after much bitterness, Cotter's Union was crushed, having gone through funds of approximately £100,000. Wilson's Union had always contained some members of the catering staffs, but they were mainly from the smaller ships, and not the liner men from Liverpool and Southampton.

Now there was only one Union left of any real strength, and when the largest of the remaining smaller Unions at Hull joined Wilson, the Union had become wholly national. It could be said that Wilson had now achieved all his original aims. The National Union of Seamen was in fact national; there were standard rates of pay in operation in all ports; conciliation machinery was in use within the industry.

There can be no doubt that the impact of Havelock Wilson on the organisation of seamen was tremendous. One need only look at the financial side to see how far this went. At the Annual General Meeting of the Union in 1896, the total income for the year ending 1895 was read out at as less than £5,000. At the AGM 1912, the half-yearly statement of total income for the Union — now the National Union of Seamen — was £217,106.18s.11d.

When it is considered that by 1929 there was a complete closed shop in operation in the British shipping industry, and that industrial negotiation was working smoothly through the National Maritime Board, it seems as though, disregarding whatever motives he might have had, Wilson succeeded in doing an almost superhuman task.

The full story of Havelock Wilson would need far more than a

*short article. But it may serve to give a background, or a broad
general picture, of just who he was and what he tried to do.*

For a real insight into Wilson's Union the author suggests trying to
obtain a book by Captain Edward Tupper, the first National
Organiser of the NUS, entitled *The Seamen's Torch* in which he
describes at some length the skullduggery that he and Wilson got
up to in the early years of this unprincipled organisation – even to
the extent of forming a scab miners' union in the Nottingham
coalfield during the General Strike of 1926! This dastardly action
caused the Union to be expelled from the Trade Union Congress
for the first time.

The tragedy for seamen was that it was ever allowed to creep
back in.

APPENDIX II

Excerpts from Those Stormy Years
by George Hardy, 1925, page 175:

Now I was again put on to this work after the British seamen on strike sent a deputation to the Minority Movements to ask for assistance. My first meeting with the strikers was in the Poplar Town Hall. It provided the chance to make one of the most satisfying public exposures of Right Wing leaders which I remember. We had received by devious means a verbatim report of the meeting held on July 3rd between the shipowners and the seamen's leaders. After talking for a while about the hard struggle against a most bitter set of employers facing the strikers, I held up the report and said: 'Let the rogues speak for themselves!' I began to read the Judas words spoken by Havelock Wilson at the meeting with the shipowners: 'We have come to say to you this morning we will give up that £1 at once ... without any argument, without any alarming statements about what is going to happen and so on ... we are doing the manly thing ... It is better for us to suggest a reduction (and when I say that is what we suggest, I want you to understand that is our offer) and we advise you strongly to accept it. Well that is the position. So we offer you the £1.' Sickening enough. The silence in the hall was complete, broken only by the voices of the seamen's wives at the back of the hall cursing Wilson. Worse was to come. Wilson went on:

'I am safely fixed in a place called St. George's Hall (the union head office). What does it matter to me if some fellow on a ship is cursing me and saying I should be shot?' Then Wilson suggested that a Blacklist be drawn up to keep out 'a lot of dirty toe-rags trying to upset what we are doing'. Now there were shouts of 'Traitor' but what followed stirred Wilson's unfortunate members to the height of fury: 'Now on some of the Liners, I have spoken privately to some of the shipowners ... the last two years I have been hammering at one thing quietly ... that these men on the Liners are a positive danger to the shipowners, because I can imagine if you were to have a great upheaval in this country ... and that is possible ... supposing you have a miners' strike, and you have the railwaymen and dockers come in ... then you would have this gang of men, these dangerous men I call them, throwing in their lot against your side ... When I was in New York, I had the opportunity of sampling these "old servants" as you call them. They are the dirtiest bunch of blackguards I have ever met in my life. If I was a shipowner I would be ashamed to carry them.'

Closing his remarks Wilson said: 'Gentlemen, I did not bring you here to lecture you. I came here to ask you to accept our offer.' The leader of the shipowners in his final remark, said: 'We accept your proposal because we think it may be of some assistance to us in bringing about other reductions ... it makes it much easier to accept what, after all, you will understand is only a drop in the bucket.'

APPENDIX III

The Merchant Ship and its Organisation

Ships of most types would normally have Deck, Engine-room and Catering Departments, each with its chief who was responsible to the Master. In the passenger ships, the Purser would be at the head of the Catering Department. It was not necessarily true that each head of department was of equal importance; they complemented one another, and all were essential to the efficient running of the ship.

Deck Department

The Master was primarily a navigator and the way to command was possible only by way of the deck department. Although 'Captain' was used as a form of address, the Master was technically a master mariner and had to hold a Ministry of Transport certificate which stated that he had passed an examination and was qualified to act in that capacity.

Probably his Chief Officer would have held a similar certificate also, although the law required him to have a first mate's certificate only. The expressions 'mate' and 'officer' when referring to deck officers were exactly synonymous and although the latter title was in common use, the Merchant Shipping Act Ministry certificates and other documents used the former.

The second officer had also to be qualified and to hold a second mate's certificate, though any officer could have a certificate higher than the one he was required to hold by law and most shipping companies insisted that he did so. The second officer looked after all charts and laid-off courses under the Master's supervision.

The third officer was responsible, among other things, for the upkeep of the ship's life-saving apparatus. On foreign-going ships three navigating officers – the mate (Chief Officer), second mate and third mate – were carried, and each of them kept one of the watches.

Some cargo liners carried a fourth mate and in passenger ships these officers were normally doubled in number with two officers keeping each watch. The Chief Officer was also responsible for the stowage of cargo, the ship's stability and the maintenance of the vessel, with the exception of those parts which came under the catering and engine room departments.

The boatswain (bosun) and carpenter were directly responsible to the Chief Officer and the deck crew were supervised in their work by the bosun. In this sense the bosun could have been described as a 'seagoing foreman'. Although the bosun was required to have an able seaman's certificate only, he was usually an experienced seafarer with rather more service than most of the men under him. His promotion was a matter for the Master and Chief Officer, but once promoted he was likely to keep the rank.

The carpenter was sometimes a qualified shipwright, a man who had served his time as an apprentice and was able to join his first ship as a fully fledged carpenter. The title was something of a misnomer since he may have had to do very little carpentry in the course of a voyage. One of the carpenter's most important regular jobs was that of sounding all the ballast and fresh-water tanks plus the bilges and recording their contents. He was also responsible under the Chief Officer, for lowering and raising the ship's anchors.

In the 1960s the deck department was diluted by the introduction of two new ratings, Utility Deckhand and Efficient Deckhand, because of the chronic shortage of Able-seamen at that time. These ratings were adults, and paid as such, which caused discontent among the Deck-boys, Ordinary seamen, and Senior Ordinary seamen who were climbing the promotion ladder to Able-seamen by the longer and traditional manner.

The deck and engine room crew were divided into dayworkers and watch-keepers, each of which worked a basic day of eight hours, but whereas dayworkers worked a normal day, the watch-keepers did their eight hours in two four-hour watches. Each watch was in the charge of an officer, one on the bridge and another in the engine room. In some cases, more frequently in the engine room than on deck, there were two officers on each watch, a senior and a junior, especially in thick weather. It was customary for the watches, both am and pm to be divided among the officers as follows – the first mate took the 4 am to 8 am and the 4 pm to 8 pm; the third mate did the 8 am to noon and the 8 pm to midnight which left the second mate with the midnight to 4 am and the midday to 4 pm watches. Deck watches were composed of an officer and three seamen, and for any given watch each seaman was either 'First wheel', 'Second wheel' or 'Farmer'. Each of these indicated a different division of duty and the order of carrying them out. Where there were three men in a watch, it was possible to rotate these duties so that each man had a different set of duties to perform on each of three successive watches. It was thus possible to break the monotony of watch-keeping whilst maintaining a continuity of duty, so that at any given moment there was a wheelman, a look-out and a stand-by on duty.

Engine Room

The engine room department comprised a team of engineer officers and ratings controlled by the Chief Engineer, who ranks with, but after, the Master. The main engine was but one part of the work of the engine room staff. Every service that is taken for granted in homes ashore has to come from the engine room of a seagoing vessel: electric light, heat, running water and refrigeration. In the *Queen Mary* there were 82 engineer and electrical officers and 153 engine department ratings. The *Canberra*, incorporating much automation, was served by 38 engineer and electrical officers. In the smaller cargo carriers there would be from four to fifteen engineers and a dozen or so ratings. The Chief Engineer had to hold a Ministry of Transport certificate of competency First Class and his Second Engineer was required to have a Second Class certificate. The latter kept the 4–8 watch and was also responsible for the general maintenance of the engine room. The Third Engineer, who may or may not have held a certificate of competency, kept the 12–4 watch and, where an electrician was not carried, usually maintained the ship's electrical equipment. The Fourth Engineer, who was ordinarily uncertificated, kept the 8–12 watch and was often employed overhauling the pumps and maintaining the boilers when the ship was in port. If a Fifth Engineer was carried he would normally spend part of his watch with the Second Engineer and, in suitable weather, may have been on daywork on deck engaged in overhauling winches.

Engine Room Ratings

On an oil-burning ship the fireman's job while on watch was wholly concerned with the boilers. He had to see that his burner nozzles were clean and that the furnaces were not being clogged with carbon from the burning oil fuel. He also had to regulate the fuel pump pressure and oil temperature so as to obtain efficient combustion without smoke from the funnel. The careless fireman, like the careless helmsman, was readily detected and the nature of the smoke told the knowledgeable observer whether too much oil or too much air was the cause of the trouble. There were usually three watchkeeping firemen, one to a watch.

The donkeymen, or donkey greasers, were promoted from the ranks on merit and experience, and maintained the same sea watches as the engineers. Their tasks included the lubrication of the main engine, generators and pumping out the bilges. When the ship was in port it was customary for two of the donkey greasers to take twelve-hour shifts in the engine room, maintaining steam and attending to pumps, while the third donkeyman was on deck seeing to the lubrication of the winches. Their rota was changed each port so that the overtime was shared evenly.

In tankers the pumpman ranked as a petty officer. At sea he worked directly under the Chief Engineer, servicing cargo pumps, deck valves and cargo pipe-lines, but in port, while the ship was loading or discharging cargo, he worked under the direction of the Chief Officer.

The Engine Room Storekeeper (ERS) also ranked as a petty officer and was responsible for engine room spares and stores. He also passed on work allocations to the day-workers from the Second Engineer.

With the growing number of motor ships being built, the traditional engine room ratings changed and motor-men took the place of firemen and greasers. It was the engine room which first experienced the introduction of the new technology such as unmanned engine rooms during the night watches, when all the oil and air pressure gauges were fixed to alarm bells outside the engineer's cabin, and eventually the whole operation of the main engine and the auxiliaries came under the control of a big computer console.

Catering Department

On going to sea the catering boy would find that in most companies he was attached either to the saloon section or to the galley section of the catering department. In the saloon section he would be designated as a cabin boy, or pantry boy, in the galley section he would operate as galley boy. As a cabin boy he would be allocated a certain number of officers' cabins to keep clean. In addition to making the bunks daily and changing the linen and towels on a weekly basis, he would also be expected to keep the paintwork clean in the officers' accommodation and to clean any communal bathrooms and toilets.

The pantry boy would be mainly responsible for the cleanliness of the pantry and washing of plates and utensils in addition to passing the cooked food from the galley to the pantry. He would probably also make toast for breakfast and prepare salads for the saloon at lunch-time.

The galley boy would be mostly engaged in the preparation of vegetables, mainly peeling potatoes, and cleaning the galley deck and paintwork, besides bringing up the uncooked food from the fridge and dry-storerooms. Cleaning the stove itself usually fell to the remit of the second cook and baker, or assistant cook if one was carried.

The chief's and ship's cook had to ensure that all food was prepared correctly and served presentably. He had to be a competent cook, baker and butcher as well as looking after the domestic deep freeze chambers and their contents.

Hours of labour in the galley were as follows: start work at 6 am after a 5.30 am arousal and work through then until 1 pm, with a short twenty minutes for breakfast. Take a two hour rest period and start work again at 3 pm until finishing work at 6.30 pm or later, depending on whether the last meal was Tea or Dinner. In a cargo ship or tanker the second cook and baker would prepare his bread dough usually on a daily basis, and then continue preparing the crew breakfast, while the chief cook was doing his butchering tasks and preparing the midday meal. After breakfast, the galley boy and second cook and baker would wash the galley deck, after which the bread would be tinned-up ready for proving and the desserts would be made for dinner and tea, together with any cakes and pastries for the afternoon tea-breaks. By this time, the bread would be ready for loading into the oven, thus enabling the baker and chief cook to go for a short smoko. Around 11 am the bread would be unloaded as baked loaves from the oven and the first dinners would be served to the 12 to 4 watchkeepers at 11.25 am prior to the midday repast.

An assistant steward could become, as fate decreed, an engineer's steward, or officer's steward, and in the liners there were utility stewards employed in a gang for the carrying of stores and engaged in restocking the passenger and crew bars, in addition to other menial tasks.

A second steward in a cargo ship was usually Skipper's Tiger in addition to serving all meals from the pantry and issuing all dry stores to the crew, he was also responsible for all bed linen and towel changes plus the bagging-up and despatching of soiled linen at each port of call.

The chief steward, as head of department, was responsible to the Master for matters affecting his department. In many cases his duties embraced the entire catering arrangements on board including purchases and control. He was responsible for the cleanliness of the officers' accommodation, the deployment of staff, and the submission of various records and forms peculiar to the requirements of the company. He invariably 'ran the bond', although in tramp ships it usually belonged to the Master, and it was he who fixed the prices of the duty-free goods which were on sale to the crew.

Some time in the 1960s the British shipowners, with the active support of the Union, introduced all-female catering staffs in some cargo ships. I never heard whether it was a success or not but it seemed to become defunct after a couple of years, most probably because of the number and regularity of unplanned and unwanted pregnancies which the stewardettes came home with at the end of the arduous voyages.

In a large passenger vessel the crew cook or ship's cook as he signed on was the only petty officer who was recognised by the Board of Trade. According to law he had to be on board with his certificate of competency before the ship could depart on a foreign-going voyage. He would have his own crew galley in the bows of the ship, or have a portion of the main passenger kitchen allotted to him, depending on whether the deck and engine crew's messroom was situated forward or midships. He would usually have a galley boy or assistant cook to help him cater for the deck and engine room ratings only and his immediate superior would be the head chef. All the sweets, puddings and bread would come from the baker's shop and all his meat would be prepared by the ship's butchers, so it was considered a good job.

The main passenger galley was customarily organised on the 'brigade' system, like any luxury hotel ashore, with soup cooks, roast and grill chefs, fish cooks, sauce cooks and vegetable cooks and cold larder chefs, each with his own team of assistants, plus a couple of scullions and a team of kitchen porters. There would also be a chief and second pantryman with a couple of assistants and they would have help at meal-times from bedroom and bathroom stewards who served on the hot-press during the busiest times of the meals. The second cook in a passenger liner was also known as the 'Galley Bosun' because it was he who had to oversee the galley wash-down after every meal and to see that the stoves were washed down with caustic soda at regular intervals, especially on the night prior to arrival in the UK. These occasions became known as the Galley Sports.